HOW IN THIS WORLD CAN I BE HOLY?

ERWIN W. LUTZER

moody press
chicago

To

my wife, Rebecca Anne, whose unselfish concern for others sets her apart from the value system of our fallen world.

© 1974 by
THE MOODY BIBLE INSTITUTE
OF CHICAGO

ISBN: 0-8024-3594-7

Library of Congress Card Catalog Number: 74-15337

Fourth Printing, 1978

All Scripture quotations, except those noted otherwise, are from the *New American Standard Bible,* © 1960, 1962, 1963, 1971, and 1973 by The Lockman Foundation, and are used by permission.

Moody Press, a ministry of the Moody Bible Institute, is designed for education, evangelization and edification. If we may assist you in knowing more about Christ and the Christian life, please write us without obligation to: Moody Press, c/o MLM, Chicago, Illinois 60610.

Printed in the United States of America

CONTENTS

CHAPTER   **PAGE**

Foreword   5
1. You in the World   7
2. The World: A Puzzle with Four Pieces   14

PART 1   LIVING IN THE WORLD OF PEOPLE

3. Contact Without Contamination   31
4. Those Shortcuts to Evangelism   45
5. Taking Your Spiritual Temperature   55
6. Resolving Our Differences   64

PART 2   ANALYZING THE WORLD SYSTEM

7. Those Don'ts and Dos   79
8. How Dollars Can Make Sense   102
9. Twentieth-Century Fig Leaves   120
10. A Rough Sketch of the Fine Arts   134

PART 3   FINDING GOD'S DIRECTION IN
             THE WORLD'S CONFLICTS

11. The Tensions of Doctrine   151
12. God's Compass Points Up   162
13. The Ax Put to the Root of the Tree   173
14. So What If I Am Worldly?   185

ACKNOWLEDGMENTS

The author wishes to thank Mr. Jim Mathisen and Mr. William Luck for their helpful suggestions in preparing this book. Also, appreciation is extended to Dr. Charles Ryrie for writing the foreword and offering his personal encouragement. Finally, the author is indebted to his secretary, Mrs. Elaine Bjorkman, who spent countless hours typing and retyping the manuscript.

FOREWORD

THIS IS A BOOK that needed to be written. Its message comes through loud and clear. It is a sober call to holiness and to total commitment to the Lord. And in the process, it demolishes many evangelical sacred cows of Christian living.

Mr. Lutzer, already known to many by his first book, *The Morality Gap,* turns his attention in this work to a consideration of how to be in the world but not of it. His writing is clear; his illustrations to the point; his analyses penetrating. Anyone who thinks he will see only the faults of others in these pages will not have to read very far before seeing himself.

Seldom are the aspects of true spirituality treated in as unbiased a way as they are in this book. Take the subject of legalism, for instance. How often the word is used; how seldom it is defined; how rarely it is applied correctly. Or take the matter of doctrinal separation. How should it be balanced with the doctrine of the unity of the Body of Christ? Or worldliness—which is usually described in terms of what others do that I don't approve of. This book knocks down rules and supports them, and both opposite actions are properly described.

Above all, the book is biblical. More than once, I stopped my reading to begin to debate with the author, but soon I realized he was pointing me to the truths of the Scriptures. Where the Bible does not speak directly about matters he discusses, the author is careful to be guided by scriptural principles of holiness. It is a genuine privilege to commend this book to all in the family of God who aspire to biblical holiness.

CHARLES C. RYRIE

1

YOU IN THE WORLD

Sören Kierkegaard, the Danish theologian and philosopher, told this parable: A wild duck was flying northward with his mate across Europe during the springtime. En route, he happened to land in a barnyard in Denmark, where he quickly made friends with the tame ducks that lived there. The wild duck enjoyed the corn and fresh water. He decided to stay for an hour, then for a day, then for a week, and finally, for a month. At the end of that time, he contemplated flying to join his friends in the vast Northland, but he had begun to enjoy the safety of the barnyard, and the tame ducks had made him feel welcome. So he stayed on for the summer.

One autumn day, when his wild mates were flying toward the south, he heard their quacking. It stirred him with delight, and he enthusiastically flapped his wings and rose into the air to join them. Much to his dismay, he found that he could rise no higher than the eaves of the barn. As he waddled back to the safety of the barnyard, he muttered to himself, "I'm satisfied here. I have plenty of food, and the fare is good. Why should I leave?" So, he spent the winter on the farm.

In the spring, when the wild ducks flew overhead again, he felt a strange stirring within his breast, but he did not even try to fly up to meet them. When they returned in the fall, they again invited him to rejoin them, but this time, the duck did not even notice them.

There was no stirring within his breast. He simply kept on eating the corn which had made him fat.

Today we face a challenge. It is the challenge of abandoning the security of worldly attitudes and life-styles to be free from the gravitational pull of the world. It is the challenge of choosing the hard path even when an easy one is open to us. It is the challenge of living supernaturally; it is the invitation to lose our life in order to find it.

Some of us will turn a deaf ear to our calling. Many will sense only a faint stirring within when they learn what Christ expects. For a fleeting moment, they will feel the impulse to walk in newness of life. But the comforts of the world, the pressures of their occupation, and the love of luxury will keep them bound to the earth. They are satsified with themselves. They will stay where they are.

Others of us will try to rise above their present commitment. They will free themselves from the attraction of money, status, and self-satisfaction. They will turn over a new leaf, make fresh promises, and determine to live a dedicated life. But they will not rise very high. Their dreams will lie buried beneath the fear that the cost is too great. They will walk slowly back to the security of former ways.

Fortunately, we find that others—perhaps only a few—will rise above their complacent friends. They will feel a tug toward the earth, but they will be drawn toward heaven too. They will not be satisfied by satiating themselves with the luxury, pleasure, and status-conscious value system of the "religious" community. They will turn from security to exposure, from contentment to a gnawing hunger, and from prejudice to love.

They will begin to serve one Master rather than two. And unlike the wild duck of Denmark, they will fly!

However, changing our life-style is painful, threatening, and often humiliating. It necessitates the delicate task of being *in* the world though not *of* it. It also involves an evaluation of ourselves, an evaluation that penetrates to the hidden thoughts and secret motivations of our hearts.

When we knowingly adopt the life-style of the world, we have the option of abandoning our present values to live a life of radical commitment. But tragically, many Christians have accepted worldly attitudes without even being aware of it. They cannot have their lives changed, because, as yet, they sense no need for inward renewal. They have not awakened from the peaceful slumber of self-righteousness. They have yet to realize that a person may give money to the church; abstain from drinking, dancing, and playing cards; win awards for Sunday school attendance; be scrupulous in conduct, and at the same time, be worldly to the core.

Oddly enough, those of us who have had religious training often find it most difficult to evaluate ourselves. The Pharisees, who knew the law and did their best to live by it, were further from the Kingdom than the publicans and harlots (Mt 21:31). It could be that great sinners are more conscious of their need for God's mercy than the self-righteous. Perhaps some of us have even eliminated our need of God. More of that later.

Living in the world is not easy. Take conduct, for example. A generation ago, many Christians simply assumed that certain amusements and fashions were not acceptable for them. Some churches published lists of sins to be avoided. Members in good standing conformed to the list and expected their children to do the same.

This method of solving questions of conduct had the advantage of being simple and clear-cut. The boundary between Christian conduct and worldliness was drawn with some degree of precision, and a Christian could simply follow the expected pattern.

Perceptive Christians, however, noticed some contradictions between the various sins associated with worldliness; in other instances, they discerned hair-splitting distinctions that could not be defended. Furthermore, standards varied from church to church and from state to state. As a result, many questioned whether we had found *God's* standards or whether we were following the opinion of fallible men.

Interestingly, this generation of Christians condones what the past generation condemned. Those who were opposed to television twenty-five years ago now have a set—if only in their basement. Their grandchildren have already spent untold hours in front of the tube.[1] Even ten years ago, Sunday sports were condemned; today Christian athletes—who play on Sunday—are heroes in the Christian community. A few years ago, a Christian was defined as one who saw his movies twenty years too late. Now that attending movies is no longer taboo in most places, that definition can be discarded. At any rate, neat distinctions between good and evil vanished with the horse and buggy.

Even among non-Christians a generation ago, there

---

1. According to one estimate, the average eighteen-year-old has spent 15,000 hours viewing TV. Assuming he has had perfect attendance in Sunday school, his Bible instructions would total a maximum of 900 hours.

10

was more agreement regarding right and wrong, or, at least, between what was *considered* right or wrong. Today, many of these views are being questioned and even rejected, and the black and white of yesterday has dissolved into the blurred gray of today.

With new forms of amusement being invented and with changes in the moral climate being greeted with indifference by many Christians, we cannot possibly predict what might be acceptable Christian conduct in the future. Someone has observed that time is the great sanctifier. The "sin" of today becomes acceptable tomorrow.

A factory official phoned a news bureau every morning to set the factory clocks to conform to the clocks at the bureau office. But when the noon whistle of the factory blew, the head of the bureau changed their clocks to agree with the whistle. The factory depended on the bureau and the bureau on the factory. Neither set its clocks by an objective standard. Likewise, the standards Christians accept today are often those of the local Christian community. But the standards of the Christian community are merely the product of local Christians. When we superficially compare ourselves with ourselves, since we create our own standards, we can gleefully give ourselves a passing grade. We are like the four-year-old boy who announced to his mother, "I'm seven feet tall." And he was right—according to the yardstick *he* had made.

Where will all the discussion on proper Christian conduct end? Perhaps that question cannot be answered apart from a more fundamental one, namely, where did it all begin? Surely God's standards have not changed. Why then have we become trapped in inconsistencies and contradictions? Why has no agreement ever been reached as to which list of sins is complete? Perhaps it is because our view of worldliness is too shallow—or too unbiblical. Maybe we have strained at a gnat and have swallowed a camel. Maybe.

What should our attitude be toward modern trends that hammer away at the accepted standards of the past? Does the Bible have anything to say about these matters? Could it be that we must reexamine principles of Christian conduct that will deliver us from simply accepting the standards of the world a few years later?

Questions of conduct also force us to reflect on how we should relate to other Christians. What should be our attitude toward Christians whose life-styles differ from ours? Or whose doctrinal views do not coincide with ours?

Our relationship with society presents its own difficulties. On one hand, we are not to be drawn into sin; yet we are also to befriend unbelievers. Many Christians think it is impossible to do both. As a result, they have withdrawn from the non-Christain community. They transfer to the sinner their supposed hatred for sin. They would prefer not even knowing their neighbor's name, let alone trying to love him as they do themselves. But before we wash our hands of direct personal involvement, before we shirk our social responsibility under the guise of preaching the Gospel, we must take another look at what it means to do good to all men—even to those who are not of the household of faith. Maybe we even have to rethink our understanding of the total biblical message and its implications for the social needs of today.

Jesus prayed that His followers, remaining *in* the

world though not *of* it, might not be overcome by the world. What this means specifically has been discussed and debated. Some Christians tell us that we should become more involved in the world; others, believing that Christians are too worldly already, argue for more separation. Some isolate themselves from non-Christians in order to maintain purity; others have participated in doubtful activities to win souls to Christ. A growing number work toward church unity; others are opposed to it, and a good number are indifferent. Hopefully this book will shed light on these matters.

Also, this book is a call to commitment that will rise above the humdrum of traditional Christianity. It is a call to march to a different drummer and to be out of step with the world.

To be holy in heaven will not be difficult. It will be the only life possible. To be holy in the world, however, is another matter. Here we feel the pressure of the world, the flesh, and the devil. Yet, we are to live in the world without being contaminated by it. Heaven is not the problem; it is here on earth that we face our most difficult assignment. As the anonymous jingle puts it:

> To live above with the saints I love,
> Oh, that will be glory.
> But to live below with the saints I know—
> Well, that's another story.

This other story is what this book is about: saints living with other saints in a world of luxury, pleasure, and moral decay. Living in this world is difficult enough, but the crucial question is, How can we live in this world and yet be holy? This question cannot be answered thoughtlessly. We shall consider it in the following chapters.

2

THE WORLD: A PUZZLE
WITH FOUR PIECES

A MOTHER WAS CHOOSING a gift for her son. "That's a rather complicated toy for a six-year-old, isn't it?" she asked. The clerk nodded, "Yes, it is. But this toy is designed to teach your child to live in this world, because no matter how he puts it together, it will always come out wrong!"

How true! We are living in a world where nothing turns out quite right. The cars and jet planes that have made travel swift and enjoyble have also polluted the air we breathe. Our big cities suffocate in the smog created by our own technology. Our natural resources have become depleted and our lakes and rivers contaminated.

We have put men on the moon but have not found a solution for moral decay. We have made gigantic strides in medicine but cannot stop the alarming number of divorces and the near dissolution of the family unit. Technology has given us more leisure time, but with it has come boredom and meaninglessness.

Novelist Ayn Rand, in an interview with college students, was asked, "What's wrong with our world?" She summed it up this way: "Never before has the world been so desperately asking for answers to crucial questions, and never before has the world been so frantically committed to the idea that no **answers are possible**. To paraphrase the Bible, the modern attitude is, 'Father, forgive us for we know not what we are doing—and please don't tell us!' " Like Humpty Dumpty, the world has come apart, and all the king's horses and all the king's men cannot put it back together again. As Christians, our tension is compounded because we are citizens of heaven as well as the world.

The term *worldliness* is often used to describe attitudes and conduct that are opposed to God's will. James wrote that friendship with the world is hostility toward God (Ja 4:4). Christians are in the world but are not to be like the world (worldly).

In order to shun worldliness, we must know what it is and what it is not. Are those who are concerned about ecology worldly? What about the fine arts: what place should they have in the Christian's life? Should worldliness be defined in terms of *what* we do, *why* we do it, or both? We can only begin to grapple with such questions when we sort out the pieces of the world's puzzle.

To clarify our thinking, we must distinguish between three uses of the word *world* in Scripture. Sometimes it refers to this planet and therefore has implications for ecology and aesthetic beauty. The same word is also used to refer to the whole human race. This relationship to the world of people is crucial in pinpointing our role in Christian living. Then often, the word *world* refers to the system of values and attitudes accepted by a society which has abandoned God. These distinctions will help us identify what part of the world we should hate, what part we should love, and how we can distinguish between the two.

When God created the world (planet), He pronounced it "good" (Gen 1:10). We cannot visualize what the earth looked like initially, but we know that it was both beauitful and adequate for the physical needs of people and animals. When Adam was created, God gave him authority over the earth with its animals and vegetation. After sin entered, God did not revoke man's authority. Today mankind has a legitimate right to rule over the earth and to use it for his comfort, food, and enjoyment.

This original mandate is directly related to the ecological crisis we face today. Christians often display little concern about our ecological problem because the coming of Christ is believed to be near. Since the present world is only temporary, it would seem that a lack of concern is justified. But is it? What is implied by the command God gave to Adam? Do we have license to do as we wish with the earth, or should we be concerned about the use (or misuse) of natural resources?

One member of a televised panel discussion stated flatly, "Our ecological crises can be blamed on the Bible. God gave man authority over the earth—authority to squander its resources." He went on to say that the answer to our ecological dilemmas is to realize that nature is, in fact, God. Presumably, if the world is but an extension of the essence of God, then man will respect nature. To hurt nature will be to hurt God.

Is pantheism (the doctrine that nature is God) the answer to man's tendency to misuse natural resources? Albert Schweitzer believed that nature was God and, as a result, refused to kill flies and mosquitoes. He saw clear-

16

ly that if nature is God, he had no right to fight nature. If he had been more consistent, he would not have killed germs either.

The pantheist faces the problem raised by Albert Camus in his book, *The Plague*. In the story, the rat-catcher faces a dilemma: if he joins the doctors and fights the plague, he fights against God; if he does not fight the plague, he is not being humanitarian. The pantheist cannot fight the plague. Remember, to fight nature is to fight God.

Furthermore, if there is no personal God, then nature is only the product of time plus chance. It is the result of blind and unintelligent forces acting together without aim or purpose. If this be so, why should we treat a tree—or, for that matter, a person—with dignity? Pantheism cannot be the answer to our ecological crisis. It cannot tell us why we should fight nature's harmful side, nor can it give us a reason to treat any part of nature with respect.

The biblical view of creation puts ecology in proper perspective. God's command to Adam did not give him license to treat the earth with disrespect. Man was made a steward over the earth and, therefore, is responsible for how he takes care of his environment. The earth remains God's possession. Man was appointed caretaker until Christ comes to rule it as God directs. Man is, therefore, accountable to God for the temporary mandate given him. As with the gifts of life, money, and time, man will answer to God for his stewardship of the earth.

Concern about ecology is not worldliness; it is wise stewardship. But our concern becomes misguided when it overshadows the weightier matters of God's will. Non-

Christians can also lead the fight against pollution and the careless use of the earth's resources. Ecology should not be primary but secondary. It is a part of God's plan for us but only a part. To give it its rightful place, we should personally and corporately do whatever we can to prevent the misuse of God's earth. We cannot ignore the earth without slighting its Maker.

However, there is another aspect of the world that should be higher on our list of priorities than the resources of this planet. It is more important than rivers, trees, and clean air. When we love this aspect of the world, we love what God loves.

THE WORLD OF PEOPLE

Charles Schulz, in his comic strip, "Peanuts," pictures Linus asking Charlie Brown, "What do you plan to be?" He replies, "A doctor." Linus responds, "You can't be a doctor because you don't love humanity." Charlie Brown is taken by surprise. "I do love humanity; it's just people that I can't stand!"

I can identify with Charlie Brown. Being concerned about humanity is one thing; loving people is another.

A few years ago, I promised myself that I would never become the pastor of a church, because I was frightened at the prospect of facing real problems. Teaching in a college was easy: almost all of the answers could be found in textbooks. But shattered marriages, discipline problems, and personality clashes were in a different category. There are no quick solutions to human needs, yet helping people is what followers of Christ are to do.

So I'm learning. I'm learning that God often calls us

to do the impossible (like being a pastor, for instance!); I'm learning that difficulties in our lives and the lives of others are designed to teach us the need for rich qualities of character and love.

Christ's primary concern is for the world of people. It is this world we should love supremely, but it's not easy.

I do not find it hard to like the neighbors who live next door to us. They are trustworthy, kind, and quiet. They never meddle in our affairs, and we return the compliment. However, as yet I don't love them as myself. There is plenty of room for improvement.

It is even harder to love those who keep us awake at night or pester us with frequent visits. Sometimes, love becomes more difficult in proportion to the amount of contact we have with certain friends or enemies. Even obnoxious friends can be loved if they visit us only once a year. Yet Christ said we are to love both our neighbors and enemies, maybe because He realized they were often the same people!

Consider this: could you love someone who killed your wife and father? Jim Joon-gon did. He pleaded with a judge to spare the life of the Communists in Korea who committed the murders, because, "The Lord, whose I am and whom I serve would have me show mercy to them." Later, he led them to Christ. That is love.

Christ did not die for a select few but became the sacrifice for the sins of the whole world (1 Jn 2:2). God loves the Communists, Nazis, Democrats, and Republicans. He loves the world.

Friends and relatives who appreciate us are easily loved; but to love those who hate us is asking too much, especially if they dislike us for no apparent reason. Yet

Christ asked the penetrating question, "For if you love those who love you, what reward have you? Do not even the tax gatherers do the same?" (Mt 5:46). His point is clear: we can love those who love us and yet be distinctly worldly. There is nothing unique about loving those who attend our church or those who compliment us for our ingenuity. That kind of love exists in all societies, Christian and non-Christian alike. To love without receiving love in return, to love without racial prejudice, to love our enemies, that is what Christ demands.

When we think of God's love for the world, we often imagine that His love is directed to an undifferentiated mass of humanity. It is hard to grasp the notion that each of the more than three billion people in the world is loved personally. We are not cards in a giant computer.

My wife and I, with some friends, were driving past a cemetery. "My husband and I bought our grave plots over there," the woman said, pointing beyond a grove of trees. Then she added, "Do you think that God will remember where we are buried in the day of resurrection?" This woman was not seriously questioning God's knowledge nor His ability to remember. She was looking for the reassurance that she meant something—something very important—to God. In our depersonalized society, people have the need to feel loved, wanted, and remembered. Christ, the Good Shepherd, calls His own sheep by *name* and leads them out (Jn 10:3). The personal element is always there.

That is the pattern for our love for others. Each of us needs the assurance that someone cares about *us*. Children deprived of love often display emotional stress or follow deviant behavior patterns. Adults who are un-loved experience futility and hatred toward society. Many are incapable of showing love themselves, yet they need someone to love them without expecting anything in return.

I have found that loving others takes effort and time If each one of us would determine to go the first mile (not to mention the second) for someone else each week, this could be the beginning of meaningful involvement in the lives of others.

Try to remember that to despise people is to despise God. Whether we are in the world or of it can largely be determined by our response to our neighbor—especially the neighbor who has wronged us.

The implications of concern for others will be spelled out in later chapters. For now, we should remember that when we serve people, we have the opportunity to serve God. If, like Charlie Brown, we love humanity in general but dislike people in particular, we have not become properly adjusted to the world.

God loved the world. Go thou, and do likewise.

THE WORLD SYSTEM

Two thieves who broke into a clothing store had a bit of fun before their successful escape. They rearranged the price tags on many of the items for sale. The next morning, customers noticed that suits were priced at five dollars each and shoes were one-hundred-fifty dollars. The thieves could not change the value of the merchandise easily, but changing the price tags was relatively simple.

What is worldliness? It is living with warped values.

At its worst, it is assigning value to what God totally condemns; at its best, it is rearranging the price tags to suit our fancy. It is rejecting God's priorities for our own. Here are three of the most common areas where God's priorities are replaced by ours.

The first is the area of sensual pleasure. God has made provision for the fulfillment of sexual drives within marriage. Yet in our society, sexual fulfillment is given such emphasis that sexual restraint is viewed with suspicion. Movies, books, and sleek magazines continually suggest that the answer to boredom and meaninglessness is to have an affair with a good sex partner. Marriages fall apart because one partner believes that he (or she) is missing out on some sensual pleasure that a different sex mate would bring. Yet those who buy this theory never find that ultimate fulfillment which our sex-saturated society promises.

God's plan is that sex should be part of life but should not be the primary criterion for happiness. Many happy marriages exist without sexual enjoyment as the basis. Single adults without sexual experience are able to live happy and meaningful lives, as the apostle Paul suggested (1 Co 7:8).

Before Adam and Eve sinned, God blessed the sexual relationship. The first sin was not the sex act, as some theologians have suggested. Sex under God's control has His full approval. But sin distorts the drives created by God. Love turns to lust. Monogamy turns to polygamy, and freedom turns to sensual slavery.

The lust of the flesh, a characteristic of worldliness, refers to any sensual pleasure severed from God's control. That pleasure can be overt, or it can be only in the mind. Worldliness is not only doing what is forbidden but also wishing it were possible to do it. One of its distinctives is mental slavery to illegitimate pleasure. Worldliness twists values by rearranging their price tags.

The second area is a direct violation of the tenth commandment. Listen to any casual conversation in a store or at a lunch break, and you will discover that the discussion is usually about money or the things that it can buy. The topic usually is new clothes, cars, furniture, or houses. What one person buys another covets.

Almost all advertising is based on covetousness. The ads feature glamorous young women and handsome men to convince us that we can be as happy as they are if we buy a certain product. Beyond this deception, there is an even more subtle philosophy, namely, that we should not be happy with what we have. To the advertising industry, being content is a cardinal sin. If we are satisfied with our present vacuum cleaner, we will not buy a new one. So we are bombarded with advertisements designed to make us dissatisfied with our black-and-white TV, our outdated lapels, and our favorite mouthwash.

The mass media has made us conscious of our own peculiarities. We are told which styles are in and which ones are obsolete. The hallmark of the advertising industry is conformity: everyone should wear the same clothes, drive a late model car, and drink the same cola. Soon we begin to compare ourselves with others who have more than we (that's more popular than comparing ourselves with those who have less). As a result, we are dissatisfied, status-conscious, and ungrateful. Our relationship with God is choked, and we are hooked on the world.

Covetousness is so subtle because we do need money, cars, and clothes. Furthermore, luxuries are not sinful in themselves. Therefore, we easily justify our greed under the legitimate guise of "making a living."

There is another side to covetousness. It involves being ungrateful for what we have. Complaining about our lot in life might seem quite innocent in itself, but God takes it personally. When the Israelites resented the desert and the quality of their food, they directed their criticism to Moses, but the Lord said it was really a complaint against the Almighty Himself.

When we are not content with what we have, when we envy those who have more than we, we have adopted the attitude of the world. Covetousness is a trademark of worldliness. It puts a high premium on second-rate values.

The third area where our worldliness corrupts the way God meant us to be is our self-image. God created us with the need to feel wanted and accepted among our friends. But sin perverts all facets of our value system. Legitimate needs are twisted into illegitimate passions. So it is with what the apostle John calls the pride of life. Pride is the sin of taking credit for something someone else has done. We have our parents to thank if we have exceptional physical beauty, for instance. And since there is nothing that we can do apart from God who gives us health, strength, and ability, it is sin to think ourselves better than others because of what *we* have done.

Let us suppose that we are successful but our neighbor is not. Or let us assume that we have more ability, intelligence, and influence. Do we consider ourselves more worthy of God's blessings? That is pride.

In contrast, humility is not deceitfulness regarding what God has given to us. Humility is evaluating ourselves correctly; it is knowing both our strengths and our weaknesses. It is seeing ourselves in proper perspective, and if we have been successful (whatever that might mean in a Christian context), humility is consciously giving all of the credit to God.

Humility is characterized by personal security; it means that we will not be jealous of other people's success or resentful if they do in one year what we could not achieve in five. A humble person will never find fault with another simply to satisfy the desire for personal gratification. Nor will he refuse to become involved, under the pretense of being inferior.

On the other hand, pride produces insecurity. It magnifies the desire for recognition and influence and enlarges personal ambition beyond reason. Pride demands that we get even with those who have wronged us; it turns love into bitterness.

Whenever we pretend to be what we really are not, or when we are motivated by the insatiable thirst for recognition, we have been gripped by the pride of life. The legitimate need for acceptance has been turned into the bondage of selfish desire.

PUTTING IT ALL TOGETHER

Think back over the three worlds we have talked about. When God created Adam and Eve, they were to be properly adjusted to these three aspects of the world. God commanded Adam to take care of the garden and to have dominion over the earth. Man was meant to subdue, or control, this *planet*.

God also provided a wife for Adam, because he was a social creature who had to have companionship. In the person of his wife and later his children, Adam was introduced to the world of society.

After Adam and Eve ate of the forbidden fruit, their world received an added dimension. Sin warped their attitudes and twisted their desires. The world as a system was born.

Yet another devastating consequence also resulted: man was cut off from God. No longer could Adam walk with the Almighty in the cool of the day. In a word, man was lost.

Ever since that day in Eden, we have tried to adjust to the three aspects of the world, but we cannot do so on our own. To be adjusted to our surroundings, to be rightly related to society, and to be delivered from our sinful impulses, require supernatural help.

Therefore, the fourth piece of the puzzle is our spiritual world—the vacuum in our spirits which can only be filled by the Creator. Whether we are worldly or not depends on what (or who) satisfies the deep needs within us. Is it God? Or our own ambitions?

Worldliness is excluding God from our lives and, therefore, consciously or unconsciously, accepting the values of a man-centered society. Sometimes it involves committing overt sins for immediate gratification, but more often, for Christians, it simply means living as though this world—*our* world—is all that matters. It is letting our job, leisure time, home, and church rotate around our special interests, pleasures, and secret satisfactions. It is spending our time to serve ourselves rather than others; it is arranging our priorities with ourselves in mind; it is living as though God does not really matter in everyday life. It is changing God's price tags.

Worldly attitudes never lead us to where we think we are going. We seek pleasure but are not happy; we buy things but are never satisfied; we attain success but do not find fulfillment.

Ironically, we are able to find what we seek if we look for it in a different direction. When we seek first the Kingdom of God and righteousness, fulfillment comes as a by-product of our love for God. And that satisfaction is better than we ever imagined. God can make the pieces of this world's puzzle fit together; He helps us view the world from a new perspective.

If worldliness is living with wrong attitudes and values, the cure is to rearrange our priorities to comply with God's blueprint. Living within the world without being contaminated by it will involve negative laws as well as positive commands. It will take wisdom, determination, and supernatural power. Our present schedules might have to be altered and our desires changed.

In order to narrow the scope of this book, I have omitted any further discussion of our relationship to the world as a planet. The rest of this book is an attempt to discuss our relationship to (1) the world of people, (2) the world system, and (3) God.

PART I

Living in the World of People

3

CONTACT WITHOUT CONTAMINATION

IN THE MIDDLE AGES, monasteries were built to keep the monks separate from the influence of the world. The theory was that if they did not associate with those who sinned, then they could attain holiness.

To a limited degree, this notion is still alive today. Christian parents often assume that their children will escape the evil of the world by being kept from knowing about certain sins or by attending a Christian school where evil is less common. Without question, this has some merit. In the Old Testament, God commanded the Israelites to be physically separate from the Canaanites, lest the nation follow strange gods. But those who have depended on a Christian environment to produce holiness (and thereby negate the evil influence of the world) have often been rudely awakened by the realization that spirituality is not automatically produced by Christian surroundings any more than motorcycles are transformed into cars by being put into a garage. Something more fundamental must take place in an individual's life in order to become holy. A Christian environment should encourage godliness, but it cannot guarantee it.

The other extreme is to assume that we must participate in all the activities of non-Christians in order to share the Gospel with them. Some Christians think it is necessary to drink liquor to witness to an alcoholic; others attend movies or read literature of questionable moral content in order to relate the biblical message effectively to the needs of today. One Christian girl planned to become a bunny (of Playboy fame) in order to win other bunnies (presumably).

How can we find a balance—if there is one—between the two extremes? What is separation all about? Perhaps the life of Christ provides a clue to true separation. Of His followers, He said, "They are not of the world, *even as I am not of the world*" (Jn 17:16, author's italice). As He *was,* so we *should be.*

PERSONAL INSULATION

Regardless of how we define Christ's separation from the world, one fact is clear: He did not separate Himself from human beings and their needs. Nor did He limit His concern to the spiritual part of man's personality. When He saw the multitude, He was moved with compassion toward them. He not only saw the value of their souls but saw their physical and emotional needs as well (Mt 9:35-36). Christ was concerned about the *whole* person, and His words matched His actions.

Christ displayed love by healing numerous people. He did not merely give them the Gospel and then move on to His next appointment, but rather He used physical healings as an illustration of the goodness of God in granting forgiveness, pardon, and peace (Mk 2:10).

In the parable of the good Samaritan, Christ commended the Samaritan for making an effort to help the wounded stranger. If the Samaritan had been concerned about souls and not bodies, it would have been possible for him to rationalize (as the priest and Levite did) and decide that he too should pass by on the other side. But unlike the religious leaders, the Samaritan realized that loving one's neighbor means helping a stranger who has been wounded—even when it is risky. Evidently, the Samaritan did not try to explain his religious beliefs to the wounded man (at least Christ does not mention that in the parable); yet the Samaritan was commended for helping a man physically and not spiritually. A man's body is important in the sight of God, and our response to others in their physical need becomes the real test of loving our neighbors as ourselves.

Obviously, the message of salvation would have been meaningless to this beaten man if it had come through the lips of the priest or the Levite, who did not care about his aches, pains, and wounds. Certainly the primary responsibility of the Christian is to share the Gospel and make disciples of all nations. But this will not be done—nor can it be done—by those who share the Gospel verbally but show no concern for individuals as *whole* persons. People respond more readily when they sense that someone is concerned about their physical and emotional needs. This prepares them to accept the spiritual dimension of the Christian message. If we treat non-Christians as if they are unimportant but their soul (the invisible, intangible, and elusive part of them) is important, they will not believe that we are really concerned about them. They will suspect that we have befriended them only for "religious" purposes, which may drive them away from the Gospel message. A genuine concern for their mental, emotional, and physical well-being can be the means God will use to draw them to Himself.

Christ also disregarded social barriers. In the parable of the good Samaritan, He deliberately chose to honor a man of a despised race. In fact, when Jesus asked the young lawyer, "Which of these three do you think proved to be a neighbor to the man who fell into the robber's hands?" (Lk 10:36), the lawyer evidently despised the Samaritans so much that he refused to mention the name *Samaritan* and simply replied, "The one who showed mercy toward him" (v. 37).

Christ could have avoided Samaria as the religious leaders of his time did, but He did not show partiality. Unlike some churches, His ministry was not segregated; He deliberately went out of His way to make sure of it.

It is much easier to talk about the unity of the Body of Christ than to practice it. Yet the uniqueness of the Christian Church should be its loving unity despite racial and economic diversity. When Christians choose a church because of its racial or social atmosphere, they are adopting the attitude of the world. The fact that a group of white middle-class Republicans is able to get along together is not really unique. Lodges and community clubs are able to coexist with those who share the same background and social status. But the Christian Church was designed to have unity despite color, race, or differing income levels. It is a pity that secular social organizations have often been more willing to accept minority groups than some Christian churches.

Christ did not respect social status. He never courted the rich. In fact, the opposite was true. The rich came to Him (Mt 27:57, Mk 10:17-22), but He went to the poor (Mt 11:5; Mk 12:37). In the book of James,

34

worldliness is explicitly defined as an attitude of personal favoritism (1:27; 2:1). In some churches, those dressed in expensive clothes were treated with greater respect than the poor dressed in rags. James reminds his readers that God chose the poor of this world to be rich in faith and heirs of the Kingdom. Then he adds, "If you show partiality, you are committing sin and are convicted by the law as transgressors" (2:9).

Tragically, we frequently live as if God is running a mission only for the middle class. It is much easier to minister to people who can earn a respectable living, dress nicely on Sundays, and live in an acceptable home—preferably in a suburban neighborhood. It is always more difficult to relate to the poor, uneducated, and racially mixed groups. But such barriers were not a part of the ministry of Christ. If the church is the salt of the earth, that salt must be found in all strata of society and among all ethnic communities.

In the book of Acts, the early church refused to associate with Gentiles. In order to rid them of such partiality, God had to use drastic measures. Peter was given a vision to coincide with the angel's visit to Cornelius (Ac 10:9-33). After he understood its significance, Peter risked his reputation to go to those dogs (as the Gentiles were unaffectionately called), even though it was considered unlawful (v. 28). Gentiles can be grateful that Peter persuaded his generation that the Gospel was for us. His words should be burned upon every heart and written in large letters on the outside of every church: "I most certainly understand now that God is not one to show partiality, but in every nation the man who fears Him and does what is right, is welcome to Him" (Ac 10:34-35).

This concept is difficult to grasp. In India and a number of other countries, children are starving, diseases are decimating the population, and war is ravaging the countryside. Is God really as interested in each of those children and adults as He is in us? Are the hairs of their heads numbered as well?

As Americans, it is easy to unconsciously assume that God has blessed us with more food than we can eat, more luxury than is good for us, and more money than any other country, simply because we are better—more important—to the Almighty. Praying for our daily bread is out of the question. He gives us this day (and every day) our daily bread—and more.

Such feelings of superiority come under the same condemnation as the Pharisees received, who thanked God that they were not like other men who deserved the fate that came upon them. But because they did not repent of their pride, they were excluded from God's program. And if God spared not the natural branches, what about us?

Furthermore, Christ went out of His way to associate with people directly. The Pharisees criticized Him for eating with publicans and sinners (Mt 9:10). Christ went to eat with Zaccheus, a despised tax-collector. All of this brought the wrath of the religious crowd upon Him. Christ defended His actions by reminding them that He had come to seek and to save the lost, and that those who were whole did not need a physician but rather those who were sick (Mt 9:12). He also knew that the poor, the social outcasts, and those who had sinned greatly would be more responsive to His ministry. Having been forgiven much, they loved much. The religious elite did not respond, because they were righteous in themselves and did not think they needed His help. Christ therefore warned, "Truly I say to you that the tax-gatherers and harlots will get into the kingdom of God before you" (Mt 21:31). Such sinners did not have to be rebuked for their sins, they were already conscious of the need for forgiveness.

This clarity of purpose and lack of hypocrisy should also be characteristic of us His followers. Christ did not tell sinners He loved them (at least, there is no such remark in the gospels), but He demonstrated His concern by personal involvement. The people knew that He loved them; He did not have to say it.

Yet, when Christ was in contact with the sinful society of His day, He Himself remained uncontaminated. His sinlessness was not impaired because He ate and drank with sinners. Nor did His sinlessness prevent Him from association with sinners. There is no evidence that He cringed when He was in the company of evil men. He was able to love them, and they responded. But the religious leaders were different. Their hypocrisy and self-righteousness frequently stirred Christ to anger and bitter denunciation.

What does this mean for us? Our separation from the world cannot be isolation from sinful society. The reverse is true. We, like Christ, must associate with non-Christians so that they will see our good works and glorify our Father who is in heaven (Mt 5:16). And just as Christ revealed the Father by His life and teaching, we now have the same responsibility. The world should look at us and see the reflection of God. We are not Deity as Christ was, but as Christ is permitted to live Himself through us, His character (the fruit of the Spirit) is reproduced in us. God's program that truth should be displayed in human form is still in effect. Except now, it is embodied in the lives of countless Christians who share the life of Christ and are part of His Body on earth—members of His flesh and bones (Eph 5:30).

Some say we cannot follow the example of Christ in associating with sinners. He was incapable of sinning, but we are liable to succumb to temptation. Undoubtedly, any contact we have with the world involves some risk. Christ has not called us to safe living. We are as sheep in the midst of wolves. God does require that we live righteously in the midst of a sinful, wicked, and adulterous generation. In fact, our ability to remain pure in the middle of a virtual Sodom and Gomorrah becomes the basis for proving the power of Christ to the world. History has shown that Christianity made a great impact on the Roman world because Christian families resisted the pressure of the sensual paganism of the day. The ultimate test for Christianity is purity within the pressure cooker of a sinful society, not isolation from it.

God called Abraham from Ur to live in Canaan, which separated him from his family but not from sinful influences. Archaeological exploration has shown that Canaan was extremely wicked. Every conceivable form of moral perversion was rampant. Whether Abraham could live a pure life there was the test of his devotion to God.

The fact that such surroundings are dangerous can be seen from the life of Lot. He was weighed on the scale of moral temptation and found wanting. His environment forced him to make the ultimate choice of whether he would serve God or pleasure. If he had been isolated from Egypt and Sodom, he might have made the same basic choice, even though it would not have been so dramatic—nor so sinful. His environment contributed to his sin, but in actuality, it brought out what already was in his heart. His choice of the best pastureland showed that even before moving to Sodom, he was hooked on the world.

We face a choice: should we pessimistically retreat from sinful society, or should we optimistically penetrate it with a wholesome life and witness? Should we be discouraged by the toboggan slide of moral relativism, or should we use it to prove that our love for Christ is greater than the enticement of the world? If we choose the latter (as I hope we will do), we will need supernatural resources to cope with the temptations that plague us.

But a warning is necessary! We cannot let sinful surroundings lead us into sin. And since we are all susceptible to sin, there are times when we will have to withdraw from people who would encourage us to follow their ways. We must influence them to turn to God; we cannot let them influence us to turn to the devil. A boy who bought a canary decided to put it in the same cage as a sparrow, hoping that the sparrow would learn to sing like the canary. After three days, he shook his head and remarked, "The sparrow does not sound like the canary; the canary sounds just like the sparrow."

When a sinful society begins to influence us, it is time to separate ourselves from it. When we begin to compromise our standards and to enjoy the pleasures of sin, we have already crossed legitimate boundaries long ago, and have identified ourselves with the world.

I met a girl named Barb when she was twenty-five. Her expression was sullen and bitter. She nervously ran her fingers along the seam of her tattered coat as she told me her story. Six years before, she had begun working in a Christian coffeehouse in order to share the Gospel with the youth culture in a needy section of the city. Unfortunately, she had underestimated both the power of sin and the extent of her own weakness. Barb became acquainted with a young man who visited the coffeehouse regularly. She felt uneasy about the relationship but told herself that she was simply interested in witnessing to him. Within three months, they were married. And then the troubles began.

Her husband was on drugs and eventually became a pusher. They traveled from city to city, spending the night in flophouses along the way. Under the constant pressures of the trade, Barb began to take drugs too and eventually ended up in a hospital. Her husband quickly deserted her and lived freely with a variety of other girls. Later, Barb discovered she was pregnant.

Emotionally she could no longer cope with reality. The trauma of drugs and the nightmare of a wrecked marriage were too much to handle.

Here was a girl who had memorized Scripture in Sunday school, who had come to know Christ personally, and had dedicated herself to reaching others. Yet now she was (and is) a mental wreck. In her words, "There is no way out for me; not even God can solve my problems." Her frantic parents have asked a thousand times, "How far should we go in trying to win the world?" A good question.

We can enjoy the company of non-Christians and share mutual interests, but often we must say a polite "no thanks" to their suggestions. Furthermore, we may have to withdraw from them completely, if we sense that they could lead us astray. To keep ourselves from such a fate, let us briefly consider the warning from God's word.

The Scriptures are filled with warnings about the danger of going the way of the crowd. Those who are weak in their faith or who find it difficult to resist the sinful pleasures of others should be especially careful in choosing their friends. Solomon warned, "My son, if sinners entice you, Do not consent" (Pr 1:10). Then he spelled out the ruin that will come to those who join in the wickedness of a gang of hoodlums. Another warning reads, "Do not be envious of evil men, Nor desire to be with them; For their minds devise violence, And their lips talk of trouble" (Pr 24:1-2). Paul gives the same advice in Ephesians 5:5-12. Scores of passages have similar warnings. Thousands of individuals (often young people) have ruined their lives because they did not choose their friends wisely. Today they have a police record, the physical and mental effects of illegal drugs, or an unhappy marriage, simply because they became friends with the wrong people.

How do we reconcile this with the previous section, where we observed that Christ, who is our example, was friends with the publicans and harlots? The key lies in our *motives* for friendship and our basic *desires* that control us.

Let us talk about motives first. We ought to love people because each one is a unique creation of God. Everyone bears the stamp of the Creator. We should love people whether they eventually become believers or not. Our reason for friendship should be to display God's love indiscriminately.

Incidentally, when we are invited to participate in activities we cannot approve of, we should be careful to explain that we are declining because of the activity itself. We are not rejecting our freinds; we are rejecting what they do. If misunderstandings develop, we might lose their friendship. Sometimes this might be inevitable, but whenever possible, we must maintain rapport so that they will feel free to talk to us about their deepest needs.

Our desires must also be examined. Evil will always be tempting and, on the surface, exciting. The problem is that we usually slip into sin so gradually that we scarcely notice it until it is too late.

Many people think that they are capable of enjoying sinful pleasures and know when to quit. Undoubtedly it is possible to stop short of overt acts of sin while entertaining sinful attitudes and desires. But few—perhaps no one—does that indefinitely.

A con artist arrested in Chicago operated like this. He would convince a prospective customer that shares were available in a highly selective company. One hundred dollars was guaranteed to become two hundred dollars within a month. The prospect would be convinced because of the sheer volume of information the con artist was able to produce. A month later, the crook would promptly hand two hundred dollars in cash to the customer.

Several weeks later, the con artist would meet again with his client. This time, five hundred dollars would become one thousand in three months. And it did.

During these months, the client would develop respect and faith in his new friend. Wasn't his friend faithful to his word? Hadn't the scheme worked? Yes. No one can argue with success.

A few months later, the men would meet again. This time, the customer gave his "friend" ten thousand dollars which was guaranteed to double within six months. And *that* was the last time they met.

It is easy to develop trust in our ability to cope with a few choice sins. For a while, the pleasures seem to be an adequate payment for our compromise with the world. But one day, we discover that we have been taken; payments other than pleasure become due. Our trust in our ability to control sin was misplaced. We have been gypped.

Think of Barb again. She knew that she should not marry a non-Christian. She also knew that the purpose of courtship is to discover whether that friendship should develop into marriage. She knew these things but thought that she could enjoy her relationship without harmful effects. And she was right, but not for long! She had come to trust sin, believing that it would pay her dividends. And it did, though not the kind she had imagined.

Seldom do we sin for cash; usually we sin on credit. The bills do not come in immediately, but they will be due. We can sin now, but we must pay later.

The point is that if we become ensnared with the sin around us today, we should have withdrawn from it yesterday! Guidelines are needed to prevent us from enjoying pleasures and habits which are designed to lead us astray. Particularly, this is true when we become friends with those whose entire life is bent toward evil. Never underestimate the power of uninhibited desire.

We need Christian coffeehouses. We need to share the Gospel in the sin centers of our world. But when someone is morally weak, the answer is separation from friends and environments that could lead to ruin. This will not guarantee Christian conduct, but it will help. We cannot choose our relatives, but, thank God, we can choose our friends.

There are also tens of thousands of Christians who ought to become friends with unbelievers and can do so without an apparent risk of falling into sin. Think of the widow next door who is lonely, the neighbors who would enjoy a barbeque, and the assistant at work who would enjoy a game of golf. In such informal surroundings, people become open to the possibility of having God invade their lives. Friendly words coupled with gracious works will unlock almost any heart. Christianity is true, even if no one ever sees the Christian life lived. But in practice, few would ever believe unless they see the life lived. And they do not see it lived just because we say good morning with a smile.

We can be thankful that the days of the medieval monastery are over. Physical separation hardly meets our biblical mandate to be the salt of the earth. Living in an evil society can serve a good purpose. The world can either sharpen our spiritual life or dull it, depending on how we hold the blade. As Vance Havner observed, you can't sharpen an ax on a cake of butter!

May God give us the wisdom to live in the world for the right purpose. Contact without contamination is a possibility only with divine help.

4

THOSE SHORTCUTS
TO EVANGELISM

SCORES OF CHRISTIANS have never experienced the satisfaction of introducing someone to Jesus Christ. The reason for this malady is easy to find, namely, that scores of Christians have never had either the courage or the ability (or both) to give an intelligent presentation of the Good News. And since people believe only when they hear the essential ideas of salvation, we should not be surprised that only a small minority of individuals are coming to know Christ for themselves.

One of the solutions to the problem is the mass media. If professionals are given the opportunity to share the Gospel with millions on television, maybe people can be converted despite the ineptitude of "average" Christians. Whether such shortcuts to evangelism are effective will be discussed later. For now, let us consider personal witnessing.

Why are so few believers able to share their faith intelligently? One reason is that they misunderstand the purpose of the church. They believe that the method of reaching unbelievers is by inviting them to church where a professional (the minister) will lead them to Christ. A hundred years ago, this method was more successful than it is now. Today, unbelievers consider church largely "irrelevant," and the meetings cannot compare to the drama of the Sunday evening TV shows. Consequently, the vast majority of people come to church only for Easter, perhaps for Christmas, and maybe Thanksgiving. And when they do, they prefer their own church to that of their religious neighbor.

PERSONAL WITNESSING

But all is not lost. The difficulty of doing evangelism within the church has caused many evangelical leaders to recapture the biblical purpose of the church, which is to equip the believers to do the work of the ministry (Eph 4:11-13). Seminars for lay evangelism have sprung up all over the country, and Christians who have never witnessed before are experiencing the joy of sharing their faith. As a result, their neighbors and friends are understanding for the first time what faith in Christ means. The church is beginning to leave the cloister and become more effective in penetrating the world.

In the book of Acts, the apostles were noted for their preaching which got results. Peter was an outstanding evangelist who persuaded people to believe on Christ. Paul also preached effectively to large crowds. This kind of evangelism is still effective today, but it should not be used to excuse us from personal witnessing. It was the common people who began the spread of the Gospel in the first century, and if we want to witness the growth of Christianity, we will have to use the same approach today (Ac 8:1). There is no shortcut to evangelism. As effective as Billy Graham has been, his crusades cannot substitute for you and for me.

As an example of personal witnessing, consider

46

Christ's encounter with the woman of Samaria in John 4. We are impressed by the fact that Christ did not avoid those who were grossly immoral nor those who may have been on the lowest rung of the social ladder. This woman had had five husbands. She should have known better, but that did not deter Christ, who was anxious that she be forgiven. Some of us would like to call down fire from heaven to wipe out those who live in immorality. But, as we noted, Christ made a sharp distinction between a sinner and sin. This story illustrates that superbly.

Today we hear many suggestions about how to open up conversations with our neighbors and peers at work or school. Questions are often memorized and later used to begin a conversation that will eventually lead to three or four points which explain the Gospel. Surely this is needed, and every believer should be able to ask such questions tactfully. But take a look at Christ.

He was casually seated on Jacob's well, and, when the woman arrived, He said, "Give me to drink." This request conveyed a needed bit of information to this woman, namely, that this particular Jew was friendly. He did not despise her because she was a Samaritan. She felt free to immediately ask Him a question: "How is it that You, being a Jew, ask me for a drink since I am a Samaritan woman?" (Jn 4:9). Since He was obliging to her, she felt open to speak to Him. This leads us to the first lesson in personal evangelism: we must be friendly if we want people to consider trusting our best Friend. If we are unfriendly, they will reject us and our message too.

It is not enough to say that we have given someone the Good News; we must share it in the right way. In fact, people seldom reveal their deepest needs to someone who monopolizes the conversation or who leaves the impression that he is uneasy in their presence. We all have an outer shell which cannot be cracked by a dogmatic, insensitive person who is more concerned about speaking his piece than he is in us as individuals. Family problems, doubts, and way-out questions are reserved only for those with listening ears and sympathetic hearts.

Christ also showed His dependence on this woman by asking her to do something for Him. He did not consider Himself too dignified to ask a favor. He did not talk down to the woman, pointing His finger at her with an air of superiority. From her viewpoint, He was one needy human being asking another for help. Such humility invariably breaks down barriers; superiority erects them.

The cure is to learn humility by shedding our indignant self-righteous attitude. Then we will not feel superior; we will know that we are saved not because we are more intelligent or live honorable lives, but because God chose to save us. Love and concern will be the outgrowth of such gratitude to God. Others will be attracted to the Christ who controls us.

In His opening words, Christ talked about an area of common interest—water. Similarly, we must share the common experiences of life with those who are in need. We live in an unjust, unfair, and unfeeling world. There are so few who are willing to take the time and make the effort to help bear the burdens and concerns of others. Yet this is necessary if the world is to believe we are for real.

As we share how Christ has met our specific needs,

how He has helped us bear our burdens and has healed our emotional wounds, we will find that others will identify with us. They will see that we are not phonies (pretending we've never had a difficulty in all our lives) but that we have found Someone who can help us work through the disappointments of life.

We could go on to discuss how Christ aroused the woman's curiosity and pointed out her sin, but our purpose is not to provide a complete discussion of these principles. It is merely to emphasize that winning the world to Christ means winning individuals. And that responsibility cannot be delegated to ministers, missionaries and evangelists. It falls squarely on your shoulders and mine.

Let us remember that the Holy Spirit does not work in a vacuum. Many Christians pray for the unsaved as though they expect God to simply break into the lives of people out of nowhere. It is true that the Holy Spirit will convict the world of sin, righteousness, and judgment, but Christ prefaced this promise with the words that He would send the Holy Spirit to the disciples (Jn 16:7-8). In other words, the Holy Spirit would do the work of conviction through the people who received the Spirit. The Spirit works through people today; He uses the message of a Christian's life (Paul speaks of adorning the doctrine of God by our attitude, (Titus 2:10), and more specifically, the Spirit drives home the verbal message of the Gospel.

We must push this point even further. Some Christians have a burden for foreign countries. They give their money to missionaries, support their church budget, and phone their friends to advertise missionary conventions. But they do not know the names of their neighbors across the street. Nor are they interested. They feel safer this way because getting to know others—especially unbelievers—can put them in awkward situations. *What shall we say if we are invited to attend a show or share some drinks?* they wonder. Such situations are sticky, and we have to learn to handle them. If we do not, the neighbors across the street never will hear the Gospel. If they have never believed, they are just as lost as the savages of South America or the Buddhists who believe there is no God. Yet, it is hard for us to accept the fact that the mission field is next door.

It is easy to rationalize and say that we are not solely responsible for sharing the Gospel with our neighbors. Haven't they heard it—or at least had a chance to—when Billy Graham was on television? Might it not be that this nation has been evangelized because of the proliferation of religious television programs from seven to nine A.M. Sunday morning? Maybe there is a short-cut to evangelism. Perhaps the day of individual messengers sharing the Good News has given way to the day of the media. Perhaps we have done our duty when we give money to missions or send a generous gift to an organization committed to sending a Gospel tract to every home. Perhaps.

THE WORLD AND IT'S METHODS

Alvin Toffler, in *Future Shock,* reminds us that we are living at an unprecedented hour of history: we are in the middle of a massive knowledge explosion. And if Toffler's predictions are even only partially correct, we have seen only the tip of a giant iceberg. Television, computers, and jet planes are only the beginning of more sensational methods of travel and communication. Presumably, the world of tomorrow would scarcely recognize the world of today. To answer the question of how we as Christians should relate to these rapid changes would require another book the size of Toffler's own voluminous production! Here, I will comment briefly on my attitude toward only one segment of our technological era, the mass media.

Methods of communciation are, of course, neutral in themselves. There is nothing either inherently good or evil about books, movies, and television shows. It is the *content* that determines whether the medium is used for righteous or unrighteous ends. Certainly, Christians should use these methods to spread the good news. But there are some inherent dangers in such methods. One is that we have a tendency to rely on the mass media instead of personal involvement to share the Gospel of Christ. When God wanted to communicate His most complete revelation to man, He did not equip the world with stereo amplifiers and beam His message to all the nations. Rather, He became incarnate so we could not merely hear the message but *see it lived*. Undoubtedly many have been converted through the message of Christ on television, in films, and in books. But such conversions have often been disappointing. Without the personal friendship and nurture of individual Christians, the seed often falls on shallow ground. There is a response—but not for long. The sun comes up, and the sprouting plant withers and dies.

Mass communication can aid in personal evangelism and the development of Christians, but it cannot be a substitute for the world seeing the truth lived *through us.* It is easy to think that our hands have been washed from the responsibility of sharing our faith personally because of the proliferation of Christian television programs. But the largest percentage of those who watch such programs are already committed to Christ. Christ said that it would be through our good works (and not merely our good words) that men would see our light shine and glorify our Father in heaven.

There is another danger. To make the message interesting, relevant, and palatable to the world, the message of the Gospel is often diluted when it is prepared for popular consumption. Some Christian singing groups are so concerned about being inoffensive that even believers can scarcely find a clear biblical message in the songs. Ditto for some Christian films.

Communication today is supposed to be indirect, thought-provoking, and, above all, entertaining. Christians who try to equal the production of the world in these respects usually come off a poor second. This is understandable, since the Gospel is not exactly entertaining; nor is it a message which people care to hear. Certainly we should be tactful, but sometimes we are so conscious of our need to keep up with the techniques of the world system (which can appeal to the carnal and frivolous appetites of the masses), that the Gospel message loses its impact. All that the people remember is that our presentation was not as exciting as the late show.

Even religious advertizing pays only minimum dividends. One church spent more than five hundred dollars on billboards, newspaper advertisements, and handbills used for house-to-house distribution to publicize a special speaker. The result: not one person who attended the meetings did so because of this advertising. There is a basic fact of human nature we cannot forget, namely, advertising is only effective in proportion to the desire people already have to attend the publicized event. Exciting movies, intriguing plays, and sensual amusements can draw throngs from a tiny advertisement. But God isn't that popular. And only a very few people hunger and thirst after righteousness. Furthermore, many people have a stereotyped or even negative view of Christianity. Perhaps they had an unfortunate experience in the past, or maybe they heard stories that frightened them, or they may be confused because of the many denominations and sects all claiming to possess the truth. In his bewilderment, the average non-Christian is determined to avoid anything associated with God or religion. He is still a person for whom Christ died. Yet he will never come to know Christ unless some Christian shows him love, compassion, and concern.

This critique of the mass media does not mean that using the media is either wrong or worthless. We should favor new and creative methods of communication, since they aid in evangelism and the development of Christians. But often, Christians prefer these methods of evangelism simply because they are impersonal. After all, when the media is used, people can be evangelized without our getting to know them, entering into their struggles, and helping them in their need.

Often rallies or radio and TV programs are used to compensate for the lack of witnessing in the inner city or other difficult areas in our nation. But the fact is that such methods simply do not reach the people who need the message the most. Many people are so disillusioned with religion that they will never believe in Christ unless the message comes to them wrapped in a body. As Paul told the Corinthians, they were a letter, known and read by all men (2 Co 3:2). The mass media cannot be a substitute for presenting the Gospel personally to those who have little prior interest in religious matters. Individual Christians are the salt of the earth.

You may have heard that men look for better methods, but God looks for better men. But maybe we haven't heard it often enough. It hasn't sunk in. There have been all sorts of schemes to get the attention of millions with the intention of evangelizing them en masse. But with all of these technological feats, belief in Christ is not spreading as rapidly as in the first century, when Christianity swept the Roman Empire.

We are responsible for telling our neighbors the Good News. And we will be effective to the extent that we have learned the secret that the early Christians learned, namely, that the men and women who have received Christ have the power of the Holy Spirit to enable them to witness. " 'Not by might nor by power, but by My Spirit,' says the LORD" (Zec. 4:6*b*).

5

TAKING YOUR SPIRITUAL
TEMPERATURE

CHRISTMAS is a time of reunion, travel, gifts, and, for many, loneliness. It is also a time for sermons. Since history repeats itself with uncanny regularity, someone inevitably preaches a sermon about the innkeeper at Bethlehem. That unnamed man of two thousand years ago is often derided, judged, and condemned. By implication, he is classified along with Judas and a few other ignoble souls who put their scar on the history of mankind. Specifically, he is faulted for forcing the Messiah to be born in a stable.

Before we consign him to the company of reprobates, let us rethink the situation. Remember, he did not know that Mary was going to give birth to the Son of God. The innkeeper thought that Mary and Joseph were just a young Jewish couple who had the misfortune of arriving after all of the rooms were taken. Yes, Mary was pregnant, but he didn't know when she would give birth. Furthermore, his inn was full. Imagine asking people in a motel to give up their rooms, even to a pregnant woman. He could not accommodate this couple, even though he probably wished he could.

If he had known that Mary bore the Son of God, he

likely would have found a place for them. There is always room for one or two more, especially for the Creator Himself. Or so it would seem.

Let us suppose that we had the privilege of inviting Christ into our homes. Would we accept the opportunity? If He needed clothes, would we give Him some? If so, would we give Him the best? Or the worst? The answer to these questions is not as obvious as it might seem. Many Christians evidently would not visit Him in prison if He were sick, nor would they feed Him if He were hungry, nor would they give Him clothes if He were dressed in rags.

Christ taught that we do have the opportunity to help Him in these ways today. The innkeeper at Bethlehem innocently refused to make room for Christ; today we can do the same deliberately. And we do.

When have we overlooked Christ's needs? When did we have a chance to help Him but didn't? Christ predicted that some people would ask that question in the future, so He answered it Himself: "I was hungry, and you gave Me *nothing* to eat; I was thirsty, and you gave Me nothing to drink; I was a stranger, and you did not invite Me in; naked, and you did not clothe Me" (Mt 25:42). Then Christ explains, "Truly, I say to you, to the extent that you did not do it to one of the least of these [My brethren], you did not do it to Me" (v. 43). Even a cup of cold water given in His name will not go unnoticed by the Father (Mt 10:42).

In the Scriptures, hospitality is one of the key marks of Christian love; snobbish cliques are an evidence of carnality and worldliness. For example, when James defined true religion, he did not say that it was church at-

56

tendance or the ability to teach (although he would have favored such activities), rather, he defined it as visiting orphans and widows in their distress (Ja 1:27). Putting a ten-dollar bill in the offering plate once or twice a month for the needs of the less fortunate is not difficult. That is only a minor inconvenience; parting with ten dollars is painful, but not for long. Hospitality means more than these things; it requires personal involvement. It takes time, patience, and is often inconvenient. That is why it is one of the most accurate indicators of our spiritual pulse.

Of course, worldly Christians—and even non-Christians—can practice hospitality. Natural human concern cares for others. But Christianity demands a level of caring that transcends human inclinations. Christian hospitality has a supernatural quality that distinguishes it from the Red Cross, Welcome Wagon, and other public organizations. It even differs from the usual custom of having our best friends join us for Thanksgiving. Hospitality, *Christian* hospitality, goes beyond ordinary human good.

Suppose that you want someone to enjoy a meal with you. Or maybe you would like to have people over for coffee after church on Sunday evening. Whom shall you invite? Your answer could reflect your spiritual temperature. If we invite only those who admire us, if we invite only those who are on the same social level or one level higher, we may be motivated by purely human love.

Christ taught that if we love those who love us, we will have no reward, for even the publicans do the same (Mt 5:46). What, then, are the elements of *Christian* hospitality?

Christ said, "When you give a luncheon or dinner, do not invite your friends or your brothers or your relatives or rich neighbors" (Lk 14:12). He did not mean that we should never have our relatives or friends in our home; the implication is that this should not become a habit. It is easy to fall into the rut of having one relative invite another and then switch homes the next week. Or consider church cliques, where members invite only those who are within their circle of friends. Church members may find it easy to be friendly to everyone within the innocuous confines of the church building, yet at the same time they may reserve the deepest level of friendship for a select few. The tragedy is that many—sometimes the most needy—are bypassed when the invitations are passed out.

Others may cater to the rich in order to make an impression, hoping that the rich will invite them in return. James uses a similar situation as a classical illustration of worldliness. In the first century, rings were a status symbol, much like new cars are today. Those who entered the church wearing such expensive jewelry were greeted warmly and given a place of honor. The church members took special pains to make the rich feel welcome. On the other hand, a poor man was greeted with indifference. The church did not reject him; the members just did not really care if he attended or not. Nor were they concerned about his needs. James says that such partiality is sin (Ja 2:1-13).

Whenever we accept people because of their money, we have capitulated to worldly values. Wealth cuts no ice with God; if it does with us, we have strayed from

His viewpoint. God values spiritual assets more than financial; when we reverse the two, we are friends with the world and are therefore displaying hostility toward God. In fact, James says that the rich are often the ones who oppress the needy and squeeze the last dime from the poor. To court the rich and despise the poor is to be married to the world.

Hospitality, like friendliness, should be displayed indiscriminately. The path of least resistance is to like the likable, be friends with the rich, and become a part of a clique. Civic groups and neighborhood celebrations are often built on such relationships.

God calls us to a higher level of concern. He commands us to love our neighbor as ourself; to do good to all men, particularly to those who are of the household of faith. That requires more than visiting with the "prominent" families in the church, who already have more social engagements than they can manage. God's call goes beyond the present to the future; it is heavenly rather than earthly; it runs contrary to human values and inclinations.

WHAT CHRISTIAN HOSPITALITY IS

Whom shall we befriend? James wrote that pure religion (outward expression of inward faith) is to visit the fatherless and the widows (1:27). This phrase was used in the Old Testament to refer to anyone who had a need and could not repay the favor. Christ put it this way, "But when you give a reception, invite the poor, the crippled, the lame, the blind, and you will be blessed, since they do not have the means to repay you; for you will be repaid at the resurrection of the righteous" (Lk

14:13-14). Whom shall we invite? Those who come to church in work clothes. Then we should look for those who are physically handicapped and who cause us some inconvenience (the crippled, lame, and blind).

The poor may never compliment us for the decor of our living rooms nor ask about the paintings on the wall. The blind might stumble over our furniture, but they will never tell us how beautiful it looks. Yet these are the ones we are to befriend. One thing is certain: Christian hospitality is not motivated by self-interest, for if we take Christ's advice we will never be repaid for our efforts, at least not now. Christian hospitality means helping those who could never pick up the tab.

Christ's instructions are difficult to obey. Getting acquainted with strangers is not easy. For some people, it seems impossible. We feel more at home with those who know our preferences and have enough insight to appreciate us. Strangers often tax our patience, talk about trivia, and don't laugh at our jokes. To avoid such a painful experience, we are tempted to invite our favorite friends for another rerun of previous social contacts. And we call it hospitality.

Christ said that those who exercised true hospitality would be rewarded at the resurrection of the just. What He did not mention is that there are special blessings for us even now if we follow His advice. When we make an effort to get to know strangers, we will soon discover that we are enriched by their friendship. Abraham showed hospitality to strangers and later discovered that he had entertained angels without knowing it. Later, this episode is used in Hebrews 13:1-2 to encourage hospitality. Much to our surprise, we will be blessed by those who we never dreamed would become our friends. We will have learned to appreciate the words of Christ, who said, "It is more blessed to give than to receive."

PERSONAL INVOLVEMENT

All of us have a natural inclination to hide our true self from others. We may be lonely, defeated, and discouraged, yet we give an impression of confidence, optimism, and even joy. Barriers build up over a period of many years and cannot easily be torn down. Sometimes we think that other people would reject us if we acted and talked the way we really felt. Yet more often, we would discover that our honesty would probably be refreshing to them, so refreshing that they in turn would be honest with us. Yet such levels of friendship do not usually happen by accident.

In fact, it is possible that we do not know the anxieties of our best friends. When we are with them, we simply talk about the events of the day or our plans for the future. Family problems, doubts, and frustrations may be driving them to despair and we might be unaware of it.

For that matter, we can show hospitality and still not meet someone's deepest need. Even the poor may have problems deeper than hunger; the defeated may have struggles beyond the usual temptations. How then shall we bear one another's burdens and so fulfill the law of Christ?

The answer lies in establishing levels of friendship beyond the usual pleasantries. Specifically, it means developing the most important of all Christian virtues: love. Some Christians are discouraged because they have few gifts or feel inadequate. Yet love is higher than the other gifts in value; love is the one gift open to every member of the church. It is not dependent on ability, popularity, or shrewdness. The greatest path is open to the least of travelers.

Without love, oratory is worth nothing. Even the ability to move mountains by prayer or the ultimate sacrifice of martyrdom is worthless unless done with love. Love does not seek vindication; nor does it tolerate bitterness. It controls our tongues because it always believes the best, hopes the best, and endures everything. Love accepts people as they are; love can take insults without ill will.

Little wonder Paul says that love will remain after all the other gifts are gone. After sermons have been forgotten, after Christian organizations have folded, and after our Sunday school enrollment has doubled, only love will abide.

Why does the Scripture zero in on love as the greatest virtue? One reason is that it runs contrary to the fiber of human nature. Left by ourselves, we take care only of interests that help us. We show concern only when it is appreciated; we love those who love us. Or we love those who can be loved without inconvenience.

Hospitality is a test for godliness because those who are selfish do not like strangers (especially needy ones) to intrude upon their private lives. They prefer their own friends who share their life-style. Only the humble have the necessary resources to give of themselves to those who could never give of themselves in return.

Hospitality also means work. A dinner is not the product of an accident, as every housewife is quick to confess. Yet it is in such informal friendships that the true needs and cares of others are revealed. This can be the beginning of more extended concern.

Since love is opposed to our sinful world, it is here that we have the best opportunity to demonstrate supernatural ability. Love defined in the Scriptures goes beyond the boundaries of human concern, and for that very reason, it is the gift of God.

On a trip to Dallas, I stopped at a restaurant in Missouri. A conversation opened with the waitress; she openly shared her guilt and domestic problems. Twenty-five minutes later, she prayed to receive Christ as her Saviour. During the discussion, she said to me, "I used to attend a church, but they didn't care about us: we were not part of the group. And we couldn't afford the clothes they had, so we were not accepted. Why does a church exist if it doesn't love people?" An excellent question. Why does it?

The opportunity that the innkeeper in Bethlehem had is ours today. Christ can be invited to our home and enjoy His favorite meal. He can sleep in our bed, and we can quench His thirst. "Truly I say to you, to the extent that you did it to one of these brothers of Mine, even the least of them, you did it to Me" (Mt 25:40).

How is your spiritual temperature?

6

RESOLVING OUR DIFFERENCES

WHAT HAPPENS when your opinion about conduct collides with that of another Christian? Should you go to a different church? Resolve the dispute by discussion? Or tell him to mind his own business?

For example, I know a man who was converted at the age of twenty-five. Before that, he had spent long hours gambling and playing pool at a local pool hall.

When he trusted Christ as his Saviour, the first major adjustment was to abandon the game he had come to love. With his new set of priorities, he had no time for pool, which had ensnared him these many years.

Sometime later, he was invited to a Christian home for dinner. To pass time, his Christian friend suggested they have a game of pool. The new convert was appalled. He could not believe that any Christian could play such a sinful game. Yet his friend insisted that pool was as innocent as Ping-Pong or shuffleboard.

Often we have the liberty to enjoy an activity that another Christian considers wrong. We might be tempted to go ahead with what we have planned on the grounds that we alone are accountable to God for our own actions. Why should we not enjoy our liberty just because someone else seems offended?

Churches have often been divided over rather petty issues that some believers consider crucial. One group is convinced that a certain sport is harmless; others believe that it is a compromise with the world. So even though our own conscience may be clear, we cannot do whatever we wish. The Scriptures teach that we have to take other Christians into account. Both the churches at Corinth and Rome had to have instructions about how to handle sensitive questions.

A word of caution is in order. When Paul gave instructions to the churches at Corinth and Rome regarding personal liberty, he was speaking about issues that in themselves were morally neutral. By "morally neutral," I simply mean that the activity per se was not sinful. Eating meat offered to idols or living according to the dietary laws of the Old Testament was not intrinsically sinful; these practices became sin if they were done legalistically or if they hindered the spiritual growth of others.

Sometimes 1 Corinthians 8 and Romans 14 are used as a basis to discuss activities such as those which will be discussed later, questionable amusements, and harmful habits. But these activities should not be automatically classified as "neutral" without any further ado. Although we might disagree on some of the specifics, the usual list of sins associated with worldliness does have important moral implications. Certain principles of Scripture remove some activities from the neutral category and place them in the forbidden column. Obviously, when Paul talks about the Christian's liberty to eat meat or not to eat it, he is referring to a matter which of itself is not designed to appeal to our carnal nature. It is not sin of itself.

The ancient city of Corinth was a center of paganism and sexual permissiveness. Part of the pagan worship involved offering meat to the gods. The priest would take the meat presented by the worshiper and put it upon the altar. Shortly afterward, the meat was taken to the marketplace and sold for less than a comparable cut which had come directly from the slaughterhouse. When the pagans became Christians, they soon realized that idols were nothing, that the meat offered to them was not polluted in any way. And so they freely bought the meat without any qualms. But there were other Christians, weak in the faith. They remembered having worshiped some of those pagan gods and felt that if they ate the meat which had been offered to those deities, this would entangle them in their past idolatry. This group would buy the more expensive cuts lest they defile their conscience by eating meat which had been offered to idols.

The church almost split on this issue. One Christian would accuse another of narrow-mindedness: after all, an idol was nothing, so why should one's conscience be defiled by eating meat offered to it? But the other Christians would say that such reasoning approves of association with idols and does not represent true separation from the world.[1]

---

1. Although Paul says an idol is nothing (1 Co 8:4), he later asks, "What do I mean then? That a thing sacrificed to idols is anything, or that an idol is anything? No; but I say that the things which the Gentiles sacrifice, they sacrifice to demons, and not to God; and I do not want you to become sharers in demons" (10:19-20) Perhaps this sheds some light on certain games sometimes associated with occult powers. Card games, for

How can such a dispute be resolved? Paul begins by saying that a Christian is not always free to exercise his liberty simply because he has knowledge (the understanding that an idol is nothing). Simply because some believers knew they *could* eat meat did not mean that they *should* eat it. Admittedly, God has declared all foods clean, so believers should not become entangled by imposing a law upon themselves. But Christians should be willing to curb their freedom if it helps a weaker brother. Paul says there are some who do not have knowledge; they consider eating meat offered to idols as a concession to paganism. And so he warns, "Take care lest this liberty of yours somehow become a stumbling-block to the weak" (1 Co 8:9).

Remember the man who was a slave to the game of pool before he was converted? He did not have the knowledge (at that time) to see that pool is no different from any other games in principle, but because he had become a slave to it, he falsely assumed that the game was wrong for every Christian.

What does the Scripture say to this situation? To God it makes no difference: a pool table is nothing. But just because believers are free to play pool, that does not mean that they *ought* to do so. They should be willing to restrict their liberty by refraining to play lest they be a stumbling block to their weaker brother. Furthermore,

---

example, are often thought to have had such an origin. The point is that *anything* could be dedicated to the worship of demons, but the objects per se are nothing and totally neutral. Therefore, they should not be forbidden, unless some Christians did make occult associations with the practice. Then other Christians to whom the game has no such meaning should abstain so that the weaker Christians are not drawn back into their former way.

Paul writes that if our liberty causes the brother to be ruined, then "by sinning against the brethren and wounding their conscience when it is weak, you sin against Christ" (1 Co 8:12). To knowingly wound the conscience of a brother (even if that conscience be misguided) is to sin against Christ Himself.

Unfortunately this principle has often been misinterpreted. Some have felt that anything that a Christian does which another dislikes means that the Christian is being a stumbling block. Not necessarily. Christ frequently said and did things that caused offense—even for His own disciples. If He had been concerned about offending the Pharisees, He most assuredly would not have healed people on the Sabbath. Nor would He have eaten with the publicans and sinners. After all, these actions offended the religious cliques beyond measure.

Consider another example. A seminary professor whose hobby was driving sports cars was told by one of his students, "Your new car is a stumbling block to me." But this is a misuse of this biblical principle. The car was not a stumbling block; the student was probably envious of the new model, especially when he compared it to his own collection of nuts and bolts. If the term *stumbling block* is not correctly defined, it is obvious that we might well find we can do nothing at all: Christians can take offense or be hurt by almost anything because of envy. You are not a stumbling block simply because you do something which others do not like or of which they disapprove.

What then does it mean to be a stumbling block or to wound the conscience of a weaker brother? Paul uses it to refer to any actions or words which would *make him fall back into his former way of life.* In Romans,

Paul broadens this definition somewhat, although the basic meaning remains the same. The one who ate meat offered to idols may feel this is associated with the paganism of the past; the one who played pool may be led back to his former life of vulgarity and gambling; the one whose god was sports may be tempted to worship that god again if he is expected to participate. One Christian who has freedom in these matters might find that he should surrender his liberty for the benefit of another whose weak conscience can be easily defiled. The weak brother feels convicted because he believes he is returning to the mire from which he was rescued.

In summary, we can say that what is safe for one man may not be safe for another. We may resist a temptation that is too great for someone else, and, conversely, we may err in matters where they are strong. Therefore, nothing should be judged merely from the standpoint of knowledge but rather from the motivation of love. We must not only ask what we can do but rather what we *should* do for the benefit of other believers. A pleasure that is not harmful for us but which may contribute to the ruination of someone else is not a legitimate pleasure but a sin. And that sin is not merely against our brother but against the Lord Himself.

THE PROBLEM AT ROME

In Romans 14:1—15:3, Paul is even more specific regarding Christian liberty. He gives four timeless principles that should be the hallmark of all godly living. Some of the Christians in Rome had a Jewish heritage, while others were converted out of paganism. Problems were bound to develop. For example, some of the Jews were still convinced that the dietary laws of the Old Testament should be kept; others accepted the new revelation that such requirements were a thing of the past (Ac 10). Here, as in 1 Corinthians, Paul emphasizes that love and harmony should exist in the church. Then he gives principles to resolve the disagreement.

First, the weak brother should not judge the strong and vice versa. Those who understood God's new revelation of freedom from the dietary laws of the Old Testament (those who were strong), were not to judge those who did not feel free to eat meat (the weak).

Parenthetically, let us remember that Paul taught that the brother who had liberty was the one who was strong, while the one who did not have the freedom to eat meat was the one who was weak. Today Paul's teaching is often perverted. Many Christians tacitly assume that the Christian who has liberty to enjoy certain activities is weak, while the one who is strong realizes that such freedom is a capitulation to the world. Paul taught the opposite. A strong Christian will see that activities which are morally neutral should not be forbidden categorically. A weak Christian who does not understand liberty in Christ will often want to multiply taboos, still thinking that spiritual living is conforming to the right set of "don'ts." In Rome the strong Christian could eat meat with a clear conscience; the weak Christian could not.

However, it is important that *neither* the weak nor the strong should judge each other. If a person considers himself strong, he will not judge someone who is weak.

Often we hear such remarks as, "He is so legalistic he wouldn't even go to a Billy Graham film when it is shown in a theater." Such snobbishness is sin. The

70

brother may have such convictions without necessarily being legalistic. Yet, by the same token, the one who is not free to go to such an event should not judge those who do. The strong brother sees that the theater per se is nothing, but he should not judge the weaker brother who believes that his own presence there would be a compromise with the world. Paul says God has received both.

Let us suppose that you, along with a number of others, were a servant in a household. Would it be your responsibility to judge the performance of one of your peers? No. Paul says, "Who are you to judge the servant of another? To his own master he stands or falls" (Ro 14:4). Paul uses the illustration of the Sabbath to prove his point. After the Jews were saved, they could not break the habit of observing the seventh day of the week rather than the first (Sunday). What was Paul's response? "One man regards one day above another, another regards every day alike. Let each man be fully convinced in his own mind" (v. 5). If both acknowledge Christ as Lord, the day itself is not that important; rather, we must realize that our attitude is what counts. If both brothers acknowledge Christ as Lord and are fully aware that they shall individually give account of themselves to God, then we should not be so quick to judge (vv. 11-12).[2]

2. Paul's tolerant attitude here toward Sabbath observance is in sharp contrast to his denunciation of keeping the Sabbath in other letters. To the Galatians, he wrote, "You observe days and months and seasons and years. I fear for you, that perhaps I have labored over you in vain" (4:10-11). In Colossians 2:16-17 he was equally adamant. These churches regarded Sabbath observance as a fetish; regulations were substituted for the heart of the Gospel. The Christians in Rome were not under such bondage.

This problem of liberty raises the question of Sunday activities such as sports. With the advent of the television set, we no longer have to leave our house to view athletic games on Sunday. If we say that it is acceptable to watch but sin to attend or participate, we will soon be caught in a host of hair-splitting distinctions. Perhaps there is room for individual differences. It is conceivable that the Master may permit one person to be involved, whereas another should refrain even from watching sports on Sunday. At any rate, let us be careful not to judge unless some other spiritual principle is violated in the sports craze on Sunday afternoons.

The previous paragraphs should not be interpreted to mean that we should not consider Sunday as a special day of worship. Even though it is not a continuation of the Sabbath, it does perpetrate the principle that one day in seven should be set aside for rest and worship.[3] Furthermore, Christians should honor God with their money on that day (1 Co 16:1); and, above all, it is a commemoration of Christ's resurrection. With a great number of events now scheduled for Sunday, we might well decide to shun them all in order to worship God without interruption. Any competition for our time always forces us to choose for God or for ourselves. But since there are no specific commands given to tell us

---

3. Many Christians falsely assume that the Sabbath regulations of the Old Testament are carried over to Sunday and therefore have rigid regulations that govern their conduct that day. If such regulations serve as a means of discipline, then this is commendable; however, in no case should Sunday be considered as an extension of the Sabbath laws. If such were the case then *all* of the regulations which were a part of the Sabbath day would have to be carried out. We could not travel more than a Sabbath day's journey, pick up sticks, cook food, or buy a loaf of bread.

what should *not* be done on the first day of the week, we should recognize that we cannot impose our own rules on another believer. Before his own Master, he stands or falls.

Second, Paul says that the liberty of one brother should not be exercised if it causes another to stumble (Ro 14:13). We have already considered this in discussing 1 Corinthians 8. But here Paul uses three expressions to describe what might happen to a weak brother if we do not consider him in our actions. The brother might stumble (fall back into sin) or be offended (question and discredit our testimony), and he could be weakened (revert to legalism simply to defend his position against what he would consider moral license).

Rather than let this happen, Paul says we should pursue the things which make for peace and the edification of one another. The unity of the church and the strengthening of other Christians should override our desire to exercise our liberty. Therefore, it is good not to eat meat or drink wine or do anything which causes our brother to stumble.

Earlier we noted that being offended means that one is tempted to go back to his former way of life. Perhaps these three expressions—*stumble, be offended,* and *weakened*—here could be summarized by saying that we should not do anything that would hinder the spiritual growth of someone else or cause him to doubt the reality of his conversion experience. But as we said before, this does not mean that we must refrain from anything that other Christians might happen to dislike. Rather, we should refrain from those activities that impair our brother's *spiritual* welfare.

73

Third, Paul stressed the need of having a clear conscience (Ro 14:22-23). This principle applies equally to the weak and the strong. The weak brother should not do anything that he cannot do in faith, even if it is a harmless activity. If he eats meat, which is technically legitimate, but does so with a feeling of self-condemnation and without conscious dependence on God, then it is sin. If he cannot bring himself to believe God's declaration that the law no longer applies, he is doubting God's approval on his conduct and "Whatever is not from faith is sin" (v. 23).

Since the conscience is often tempered by environment, some people may feel convicted when doing the most trivial actions. Within time, they may begin to accept God's revelation regarding Christian liberty; until that happens, they are sinning if they cannot do these activities in good conscience. Let us remember that the strong brother cannot have a clear conscience even if he does what is legitimate for him, if at the same time his conduct impairs the spiritual life of his brother. And the strong brother should realize that he has the primary responsibility. "We who are strong ought to bear the witnesses of those without strength" (15:1).

Finally, Paul says that rather than pleasing ourselves, we should do all to glorify God (15:16). A widespread notion making the rounds today teaches that when we curb our liberty, we are automatically putting ourselves under legal bondage. Since we are to enjoy our liberty in Christ, some think that we are legalistic if we don't do everything we may have the right to do. But Paul clearly taught that one could have Christian liberty without exercising it. And for this reason, we should gladly conform to certain disciplines rather than hinder our brother's spiritual welfare. The strong brother retains his liberty though he does not use it. If, because of selfishness, a believer insists that he should do whatever he feels he is at liberty to do, he is unlike Christ who did not please Himself (v. 3). Christ did not do merely that which was convenient for Himself, rather, He acted for our good.

If we judge our conduct by Christ and His desire to please the Father, we will solve many decisions regarding behavior. Will my actions attract individuals to Christ? Will it cause them to use my actions as license for their misuse of liberty? And finally, am I causing division in the church because of my misuse of liberty?

These questions are necessary in exercising our freedom among other believers. Strong Christians should be the first to adjust their liberty accordingly. If playing a certain game causes our brother to stumble, we should be willing to curb our liberty for his good. Paul would have done that, and so should we.

PART II

Analyzing the World System

7

THOSE DON'TS AND DOS

"MANY OF THE STUDENTS here look at the world and think they have been gypped," remarked a coed at one of our leading Christian schools. "They envy those who are enjoying sinful pleasures." She spoke more profoundly than she knew. Many Christians resent their spiritual heritage, because they believe that life would be more fun if they had no restrictions that cramp their life-style. They are convinced that by trusting Christ as their Saviour, they have gained very little—at least in this life. Maybe it will pay off in the wild blue yonder, but for the here and now, it's a drag. They've been gypped.

Satan got Eve to believe a similar story in the Garden of Eden. He got her to concentrate on the one negative (the forbidden tree) so that she would be detracted from the positive blessings (the many trees that were permissible). In one master stroke of genius, he was able to convince her that God was withholding something good. If she would only disobey God's command, she would then be like God, knowing good from evil.

Eve believed Satan's story. God was indeed withholding something good from her. She looked with envy at the fruit of the forbidden tree. Surely this restriction was not for her benefit. God had given this command because He did not want her to enjoy life to the fullest.

He just wanted to keep her under His thumb. And so she ate the fruit. But everything did not turn out quite like Eve had imagined. The fruit tasted good, but as a result of the disobedience, a host of problems appeared. And it all began when Eve thought that being restricted from one tree meant that she was receiving the short end of the deal.

There is a fable of a kite which once said to itself, "If I could just get rid of that man who is holding me back, then I could fly above the clouds and kiss the stars." One day the string broke. Now at last, it was free to soar higher than it had ever gone before. But much to its surprise, it did not rise above its present height. In fact, it came crashing down to the ground. The kite had not realized a fact of aerodynamics: the string holding a kite down is the string holding it up. A kite can fly above the clouds only when the man on earth is in full control.

God's restrictions not only hold us down but they also hold us up. We will never achieve fulfillment unless He is in control. He did not send His Son to cramp our life-style but to give us a much better one. And if we are not finding that to be true, something drastic has gone wrong.

But how do we go about deciding which actions are right or wrong? How do we solve those stickly questions regarding amusements, habits, and life-styles?

Some acts are always sin regardless of the circumstances. It is always wrong to break the commandments which have been expressly revealed. For example, adultery, lying, and stealing are always sin and cannot be justified by the situation. Then there are numerous negative commands in the New Testament. It is always sin to be conformed to the world (Ro 12:2), to permit unwholesome words to proceed out of our mouths (Eph 4:29), to grieve the Spirit (Eph 4:30), or to be ashamed of the testimony of the Lord (2 Ti 1:8). Living under grace does not mean we are free from commandments.

Then there are some things that are always right. For example, it is always proper to love one another (Ro 12:10), to set our affections on things above rather than things on earth (Col 3:2), to let the peace of God rule in our hearts (Col 3:15), and to give thanks in every circumstance (1 Th 5:18). This list could be expanded almost indefinitely. There are scores of such exhortations in the New Testament which are the will of God for us all.

But the fact is that there are many questionable activities which are difficult to classify categorically as "sinful" or "not sinful." What about movies, Sunday sports, television, or social drinking? Is it possible to do these things without being worldly? Or should such a list be used to define precisely what worldliness is?

One Christian, who had become weary of the disagreements that exist regarding the specifics of Christian conduct, made this suggestion: a group of church leaders ought to form a list of sinful activities so that the average Christian could know at a glance what is sin and what is not. Then we could just follow instructions rather than constantly face such decisions on our own.

On the surface, this suggestion might seem feasible or at least worth a try. But a closer analysis will show that such an assignment can never be done. It sounds simple, but in practice, it is impossible.

Even if we made a complete list of all the commands of Scripture, we could not thereby solve all of the problems associated with Christian conduct. For one thing, even innocent actions can *become* sin if we are inordinately attached to them; for another, our different weaknesses make it impossible to specify appropriate conduct for everyone.

Disagreements on these matters force us to examine the basis of our conduct. We must understand why opinions have been divided on these and similar issues. Let us begin by clarifying the misused and misunderstood word, *legalism*.

THE MEANING OF LEGALISM

Frequently a Christian who lives according to certain standards and in harmony with a list of commandments is classified as a legalist. Advocates of the new morality give the erroneous impression that the very existence of laws or rules results in legalistic behavior. But in the Old Testament, God spelled out His will in the Ten Commandments and hundreds of other detailed laws (613 to be exact). If the very existence of laws constitute legalism, then God has obviously encouraged legalism in every conceivable form. However, obedience to laws does not constitute legalism. A Christian who lives within the commands of the New Testament—or even regulations he has set up for himself—is not necessarily legalistic. He may be—but not necessarily.

What then is legalism? It is a *wrong use* of laws and rules. Or, to put it another way, legalism results by ascribing the wrong function to the Law. Basically, three forms of legalism are referred to in the Scripture. First, there is the legalism of those who believed that salvation could be attained by keeping the Law. For example, the rich young ruler thought that he had kept the Law from his youth; such obedience was commonly believed to be sufficient for salvation.

Literally millions living today have a similar view. They think that God has a scale in heaven, and that if their good works outweigh the bad, they will be received with the righteous in the day of judgment. "If I do my best and try to live up to the Sermon on the Mount, what else can God expect?" they ask impatiently. They do not realize that God demands infinitely more, so much that only those clothed in the righteousness of Christ receive His approval. Legalism is the belief that keeping moral laws (or attempts to) will correct a man's relationship with God.

Second, there is the legalism of the Jews mentioned in Galatians who believed that although salvation was free and to be accepted by faith, living the Christian life (walking in the Spirit) was a simple matter of keeping the Law. Having begun in the Spirit, they now hoped to be made mature by works of the flesh (Gal. 3:1-3). This sort of legalism is frequently found in evangelical circles, where the Gospel is clearly presented, then the saved are asked to conform to certain patterns of behavior to become mature in Christ. Of course, if there is immoral conduct, new converts should be exhorted to bring their conduct in line with biblical requirements. However, as we shall see later, even this does not *produce* spirituality.

Third, there is the legalism of the Pharisees who not only tried to keep the Law for personal salvation but also went beyond the teachings of Scripture by adding their own customs to the Old Testament Law. For example, the Mosiac law forbade the practice of reaping on the Sabbath (Ex 34:21). But it did permit a hungry traveler to pluck and eat corn from another's field so long as he used his hands and not a sickle (Deu 23:25). But the Pharisees felt that plucking corn on the Sabbath came close to reaping, and in order to be sure that everyone stayed well within the prescribed limits, they felt that merely eating corn while walking through a field on the Sabbath should be regarded as sin too. Christ did not adhere to such additions to the Law and accused them of teaching the traditions of men for the commandments of God (Mk 7:7).

This type of legalism is still popular today. Christians often go beyond scriptural teaching in defining what Christian conduct involves. Sometimes this is done because biblical principles are thought to be at stake; at other times, rules are made which confuse cultural mores (customs attached to a given country or locality) with biblical teachings. For example, hairstyles and dress codes are sometimes the yardstick used to measure worldliness. Of course there are those who dress immodestly, and others are a slave to fashions. But many of our accepted standards are merely conventional. In some churches, the men who serve the elements on Communion Sunday are required to wear white shirts for the meeting. Lower standards (colored shirts) are apparently legitimate for less spiritual occasions. This shows what happens when we confuse biblical principles with social conventions.

We could clarify such confusion by listing the traditions of churches and then giving the biblical teaching (chapter and verse) upon which these traditions are based. After that, we could evaluate our practices in order of their importance. For example, Christ told the Pharisees that they had done right in tithing but that they had neglected the weightier matters of the Law, such as justice, mercy, and faithfulness (Mt 23:23). He also said that what went into a man (the outward) was not as important as what proceeded from within his heart (Mk 7:18-23). This assignment would help us see the essential in contrast to the peripheral. We would discover that we are not really becoming worldly merely because some men are growing beards and others are wearing colored shirts.

What about instances where moral principles *are* involved? Is it not logical to specify precisely what amusements, habits, and vocations are acceptable and which ones are not? This question will be discussed in detail later. For now, it is sufficient to note that the legalism of the Pharisees was not only the error of thinking that keeping the Law was all that God demanded, but they also added to its requirements in their quest for righteousness.

To summarize, legalism is a misunderstanding of the purpose of the law. It has two chief characteristics. First, it assumes that godliness consists merely of living as closely as possible to moral laws. Legalists are right in insisting that we should keep moral laws; but they err in thinking that such conformity changes our relationship with God. Many non-Christians do not lie, steal, or commit adultery. They may also abstain from movies, smoking, dancing, and drunkenness. If we define spirituality in terms of what we should *not* do, then even atheists could pass the test!

Satan does not mind if we equate spirituality with

good works. As long as he can keep us from walking in newness of life, he doesn't care whether we take God's name in vain or not. If he can get us to believe we are righteous because we attend church on Sunday evenings rather than watch television, he has won a colossal victory. He even enjoys a prayer of thanksgiving as long as it goes, "I thank God that I am not like other men who smoke, drink, and gamble, or even like this church member who drinks wine at his table." Such a person still thinks that he is righteous because of what he is doing rather than because of what God has already done. To him Christ would say, "For you are like whitewashed tombs which on the outside appear beautiful, but inside they are full of dead men's bones and all uncleanness. Even so you too outwardly appear righteous to men, but inwardly you are full of hypocrisy and lawlessness" (Mt 23:27-28).

Second, legalism emphasizes outward conduct almost solely to the exclusion of inward thoughts and motivations. Since legalists do not understand the far-reaching consequences of living according to biblical exhortations, they are content to define worldliness according to a given list which specifies which amusements and habits are sins and to be shunned. Those who obey the list are not worldly; those who do not, are.

In one word, legalism is *self-righteousness*. It is the belief that God is satisfied with our attempt to obey a moral code. The legalist lives the Christian life (or what he thinks is the Christian life) by sheer willpower and is proud of his efforts.

Now we must consider in more detail the blight of legalism, especially the type that has stunted the spiritual growth of numerous Christians. Specifically, we must see the limitations and problems connected with using a code to define what Christian living really means.

THE DANGERS OF LEGALISM

Of the three types of legalism mentioned, the second (spiritual maturity comes by the law) and the third (adding to the biblical laws) are both found in evangelical churches. Usually they exist together. Many who understand clearly that salvation comes by faith alone, believe that spiritual growth is nothing more than conformity to a list of "don'ts." And in order to make certain that everyone falls into the pattern, the requirements are spelled out in more detail than the Scriptures themselves warrant.

Sometimes those who join churches are expected to conform to certain restrictions which may limit their amusements, habits, and life-styles. Since such lists often vary from church to church and from state to state, perceptive Christians have wondered aloud whether such sins are actually based on the Scriptures. Presumably, if these so-called taboos were condemned in Scripture, all questions regarding them would be settled once and for all. But this has not happened. In fact, as the years pass, the lists not only vary but become shorter.

These restrictions originally arose because of the dangers and temptations associated with some activities. As our society becomes inflicted with sensuality, the pressure to conform to the mood of our day is powerful. So two matters need emphasis. First, I am not suggesting that we necessarily condone the activities which have been classified as sinful. My point is that a list of sinful activities should not be used to define worldliness.

As we shall see, lists have not—and cannot—go far enough. To let a list of taboos specify worldliness is being content with too little. In fact, whenever we classify a list of activities as "worldly," we may unintentionally be lowering our standards rather than elevating them.

Second, a list of prohibitions can be of value if its limitations are properly understood. Such standards can help keep us from sin. However, we err when we tacitly assume that such restrictions somehow make us righteous; we err in thinking that such a list of activities can define what a Christian life-style really is. For this reason, we must understand the limitations of outward restrictions, or else we will be guilty of reducing Christianity to a life-style which falls short of what God intended. Why?

Whenever we label certain questionable activities as "sin," there is the tendency to lose sight of the biblical admonitions which are to guide us in every area of conduct. For example, Christ taught that if we look at a woman to lust, we have already committed adultery in our hearts. This teaching is universally true; there are no exceptions. This one verse alone is sufficient to eliminate scores of books, movies, and television shows which are designed to lead us to sensual thoughts. Parents have the responsibility to forbid their children to attend amusements, social functions, or parties that foster and encourage permissiveness. All Christians should restrict themselves in those areas where they are weak and tempted to sin. Yet when we identify one or two activities as being sinful, we often give the impression that those who do not participate in these activities are ipso facto living an acceptable moral life. Yet, it is obvious that such a conclusion does not follow. We can be sensual without attending movies or watching the late night show. So, while we need not condone questionable activities, we dare not give the impression that those who refrain from these activities are automatically living according to a distinctively Christian life-style. Of course they may be, but not necessarily.

Rules can cover only a small fraction of the situations where we might be led into sin, and of course there are no rules that can keep us from covetousness and pride. So, even though certain restrictions are commendable, they should not become a substitute for teaching the radical purity of heart which Christ demands. Abstaining from certain amusements is necessary but also very easy (we noted before that atheists could do this too); however, God's standards penetrate so much deeper that only He can give us the power to live as He intended. Christianity demands more than abstaining from a few selected sins.

Another danger in using a list of don'ts to specify worldliness is the temptation to minimize our obligation toward God. As humans, we are often satisfied to fulfill the minimum that is required of us—just enough to be accepted by the Christian community and pay God His dues. When we do not genuinely hunger and thirst after righteousness, we will always want to know precisely what is expected and do only that.

The difference between outward and inward motivation can be illustrated by someone who works for an employer. If his heart is in the work, he will not look at his watch regularly throughout the day, unless it is to see how *much* he can do per hour. He does not mind working overtime if his schedule permits it. He delights to be at the service of his boss. But the worker who is there only for his paycheck wants to know the rules so that he can see how little he can do without having the wrath of his employer fall on him. When work is over at five o'clock he drops whatever he is doing. If he is asked to help out on another project, he objects, "I wasn't hired to do this."

This attitude is exemplified by the person who asks, "How should a person tithe? Should he give ten percent of his net or gross income?" He asks this because he wants to know precisely what he is obligated to do. And now that God has ten percent, the ninety percent can be spent freely. Like paying union dues, he never gives more than asked. Of course, many who tithe do not do so legalistically. They joyfully give one-tenth of their income to specific Christian ministries and use the other ninety percent faithfully, recognizing that it belongs to God as well. But we must be careful not to give the impression that the Christian life can be defined in terms of a given number of obligations.

A legalistic athlete dislikes football but plays the game to please the coach or to get a good raise. He wants to know precisely what the requirements are; he finds out how many practices he is permitted to skip, and he makes sure he uses his quota. Of course, it is better that he do the minimum of what is required than nothing at all, but candidly, he finds playing football a drag. His heart is somewhere else. Another athlete plays football for the sheer love of the game. He is not concerned about the minimum requirements set down by the coach, because he goes beyond what is expected. He does not try to see how much he can get by with and still be accepted by his teammates. His heart is in the game. Both athletes keep the rules of their club, but one is legalistic and another is not. Question: How are you playing the Christian life?

A third danger in making a list of sinful activities is that contradictions and petty distinctions are almost inevitable. Joe Bayly has suggested that God must have a sense of humor; surely He must have laughed when Christians bought TV sets to get caught up on the movies they had missed during the past twenty years. Some Christians never play sports on Sunday or attend games but will watch the football game at home on Sunday afternoon. Smoking is condemned because our body is the temple of the Holy Spirit, but one who lives on insufficient sleep is considered diligent. Gluttony, which harms the body extensively, is only mentioned in jest. Such inconsistencies could be multiplied indefinitely.

Faced with these difficulties, some Christians have mistakenly concluded that all rules should be dropped in order to be consistent. But this attitude displays a misunderstanding of the issues involved. The solution is not to approve of all activities listed simply to be consistent. Rather, the inconsistencies only remind us that it is impossible to specify consistently how a given scriptural principle is to be applied. The taboos are not necessarily wrong but merely inadequate. So rather than multiplying more rules or increasing the list of don'ts, we must return to the basic principles and show how they are to be applied in all situations. This may necessitate abstaining from certain habits, but it will also include much more. Each Christian must go beyond the restrictions of his church to determine what God expects of him personally. In some cases, there may be personal differences, but a Christian life-style must be rooted in the guidelines and principles revealed in the

Scriptures. As will be shown, principles can be consistently applied.

What it boils down to is this: can we solve the problems of legalism by changing our standards or by changing people? Perhaps if we begin to see the thrust of God's commands, we will understand why the Christian life is more than conformity to a given behavior pattern; it is more than a life lived by sheer willpower. It is a radical transformation calculated to change us from the inside out. Briefly, it is God doing what the best laws and rules cannot do; it is God giving us Christ's righteousness as well as qualities of character that transcend human ability. A return to the basics of Scripture will be a return to the living God.

Living Under Grace

Since no rules—including the moral law—can produce spirituality, some Christians conclude that it is unnecessary to be subject to any restrictions. This attitude is often found among those who have been delivered from excessive legalism. They finally realize that spirituality does not come by the law, so they have a "liberated syndrome" which makes them disdain all restrictions. Perhaps they have seen many who believed they were righteous because they abstained from the list of sins on the church consecration pledge. So when they (the supposedly liberated Christians) finally see that spirituality is produced by submission to the Holy Spirit, they misuse their new freedom. They reason thus: if spirituality is not generated by abstaining from certain amusements, social activities, or sensual pleasures, why should I refrain from these activities? On the surface, anything seems permissible. This is why Paul warned, "For you were called to freedom, brethren; only do not turn your freedom into an opportunity for the flesh, but through love serve one another" (Gal 5:13).

It is true that the entire Mosaic law, including the Ten Commandments, was done away in Christ (2 Co 3:7-11). But this does not mean that we can do as we please. In this age, we are under the law of Christ which differs from the Mosaic law in at least three ways. First, we are under more stringent demands. It is relatively easy to keep the commandment "Thou shalt not kill," but Christ taught that hating your brother means that you are a murderer at heart (Mt 5:22). We cannot solve the problem of legalism by abolishing laws! The first step in turning from legalism is to realize that the attitude of our heart must correspond with outward conduct. The Mosaic law emphasized overt sin; those who kept it outwardly erroneously believed they had met God's requirements.

Christ's definition of sin penetrates far deeper than a list of sins on a membership card. It goes to our inner desire, motivations, and secret thoughts. His teaching condemns us so completely that we can never again think that we have any righteousness of our own.

There are literally hundreds of commands in the New Testament that are humanly impossible to keep. We are called to live in a manner radically distinct from the accepted conduct of mediocre Christianity. Facing the impossible, we are driven to Christ for forgiveness and superhuman ability. God has not relaxed His standards, and neither can we.

Second, the motivation under the Mosaic law was, "Obey and you will be blessed." Today we have a different incentive. God has already freely blessed us with all spiritual blessings (Eph 1:3). Now we are to serve Him out of sheer gratitude for what Christ has *already* done for us. True Christianity can never be reduced to a pattern of behavior agreed upon by a committee.

Have you ever wondered why one characteristic of legalism is a critical attitude? The simple reason is that a legalist is never motivated by joy. A legalist will do only what is expected, and when he does go beyond the call of duty, it is to exhalt himself. His heart is not in what he does. As a result, he envies those who are getting by and not toeing the line. He resents others who enjoy activities he secretly would like to do himself. He likes specific rules so that he knows what he is obligated to do; then he has the satisfaction of knowing that he has scrupulously done his duty.

This is why there will be some surprises at the judgment seat. Christ told a parable about some laborers who had agreed to work in a vineyard for a penny (denarius) a day. But those who had been hired at the third hour received the same amount as those who were hired at the eleventh. The first group, who had worked all day, complained because they received no more than those who had come later. Yet the landowner answered, "Is it not lawful for me to do what I wish with what is my own? Or is your eye envious because I am generous? Thus the last shall be first, and the first last" (Mt 20:15-16). Some self-righteous individuals think that God is pleased with them because they have spent more time in His vineyard. They forget that God owes us nothing.

Any rewards we receive are of His grace, and even after

we have given our best, we are still unprofitable servants and have done only our duty.

A legalist's motivation is the Law; he plods along hoping that some day his effort will pay off. He prides himself in his faithfulness in "serving the Lord," even though his neighbors have seen no reasons why they should want to serve that same Lord.

Third, living under grace means that supernatural power is readily available. In the Old Testament, the ministry of the Holy Spirit was restricted; not all believers were indwelt. Since the day of Pentecost, every believer is indwelt by the Holy Spirit. The result is that we are able to have character traits that God alone can produce in us. We can obey restrictions by sheer willpower, but we cannot live the Christian life on that basis. A Christian life-style is the character of Christ reproduced in us. It is living supernaturally in a world that is convinced that the supernatural is a relic of past imaginations.

When Paul listed the nine fruits of the Spirit in Galatians, he added, "against such things there is no law" (5:23). There can be no law prohibiting such qualities; and we may add that there is no law that can produce them either!

True, restrictions can neither produce nor guarantee spirituality; but if we submit to the Spirit, we will discover enablement to meet the demands of the Law more fully than before. As Paul put it, God sent His Son "in order that the requirement of the Law might be fulfilled in us, who do not walk according to the flesh, but according to the Spirit" (Ro 8:4). When we are controlled by the Spirit, we will fulfill the Law but in a different way and for a different reason than the legalist who believes that his human effort is all that God requires.

To summarize, the good is sometimes the enemy of the best. A legalist misuses something good (the Law or valid restrictions), and this prevents him from seeing the new life Christ came to bring. The answer to legalism is not to abolish restrictions. Rather, it is to recognize that the only righteousness available is what Christ gives us and that the possibility of living the Christian life is dependent on His power. Drudgery must be exchanged for delight, self-righteousness for humility, and criticism for commitment.

Anything less than this reduces Christianity to a life that a worldly Christian can live.

LIVING BY PRINCIPLES

If the Bible writers listed which activities are sins and which are not, the Bible would soon be out of date. As new amusements and pleasures were invented, any list compiled in the first century soon would become obsolete.

But the Bible is timeless; its teachings can be applied in every age in all cultures. Its commands are directed primarily to our hearts, and in this way, it escapes the limitations of an arbitrary list of sins. Our behavior should be based on its teachings, commands, exhortations, and doctrine. Such an approach will give us a solid foundation for our conduct in a day of relativism and worldly pressures.

In a way, it is a good thing that certain practices (watching football games on Sunday) and certain amusements (playing pool) are no longer taboo. Many

Christians are finally realizing that Christianity is more than a list of don'ts. However, along with this realization, a new danger has been created. By rejecting the taboos of the past, many Christians are also rejecting the basic principles which originally gave rise to those taboos. To use a cliche, the baby is thrown out with the bath water. If an activity is now permissible, there are those who think they have the right to do it without any questions asked.

If their church approves movies, they attend the theater without exercising discretion. They never stop to evaluate their actions or even pause to ask whether the amusements they enjoy are positively helping them to fulfill the will of God in their lives. As the taboos are abandoned, they have no moral or spiritual basis for their conduct. All that they know is that what was wrong is now right, and what is wrong today may be right tomorrow. As the Christian community sinks, they sink along with it.

For example, when television was first invented, many Christians were opposed to it. Later, television received acceptance. But along with that acceptance, the principles which led to its original rejections were abandoned. In other words, when television was approved among Christians, it was accepted in toto, without specific biblical principles governing its use. Consequently, children are permitted to watch practically all types of shows; parents waste time watching worthless programs, and hours are squandered that should be spent with the family. Because the evangelical constituency was not trained to apply biblical principles to situations (such decisions were made by those who formulated the rules), television has turned out to be a god for many. Little can be said to such people without them responding, "What's wrong with television?" And, of course, the answer is "nothing." But some Christians have forgotten that such a gadget, used without a consistent application of biblical principles, can lead to spiritual disaster.

In South America, upon leaving an old Catholic church every Sunday morning, the congregation turned to face an old wall, genuflected, made the sign of the cross, and then left. A visitor was curious to find out why they did this, especially because the wall was bare. When he asked the people why they did it, they answered that their parents and grandparents had done this, so they did it too. Years later, when the church was torn down, the workmen discovered beneath the many layers of paint on that wall, a beautiful painting of the virgin Mary. The original congregation had bowed to the beautiful painting, but the succeeding generations had simply perpetuated the tradition, even though the reason for their religious rite had long since vanished beneath the dust and paint.

Some Christians copy the conduct of their friends or church. When the Christian community changes its standards, they do too, but they never know why. They are content to follow blindly the questionable assistance of others. The penetrating teachings of the New Testament have either been jettisoned or else buried beneath debris.

Many Christians object to a given list of sins, not because they want to elevate Christian conduct to the radical level of the New Testament but because they would like to lower their personal standards. Maybe they suspect that they are missing out on some pleasures, perhaps even sensual ones. So, they criticize the taboos of the past for the wrong reasons. Their convictions continually shift on the quicksand of moral indifference.

Our only hope is obedience to the teachings of the New Testament; our fate depends on whether we are willing to become one of Christ's disciples in the fullest sense. Then we will search our hearts, motives, and affections. Anything that mars our fellowship with God will be recognized as sin. We will discipline and restrict ourselves in matters that can never be included in an official statement on worldliness. Like Christ, we will not please ourselves but will want to please God alone.

What else would happen if we began to live according to the teachings of the New Testament? What would the implications be if we actually did set our affections on things above and not on things of the earth? What if we actually did seek first the Kingdom of God and His righteousness? Or what if we did yield our bodies as sacrifices to the living God? And if we prayed without ceasing?

The consequences of such obedience are devastating to someone who does nothing more than live up to a list of rules. Let me suggest three effects this perspective would have on our conduct. First, we would evaluate *everything* we do in the light of God's demands; we would be sensitive to His control in every area of our lives. Even wholesome activities would have to be abandoned when they overshadow the weightier matters of discipleship.

For example, even sports such as football, basketball, and tennis are sin when they become the consuming passion of our lives. There are those who justify their interest in such games because they derive their standards from the church, which, of course, approves of such recreation. But what we must realize is that even such neutral activities are sin when they occupy time, attention, and energy that should be directed toward our families, our friends, and God (not always in that order). It seems odd that some who have difficulty remembering even the most familiar passage of Scripture find that they are able to recite the batting averages of several players. We remember those things we are interested in. And where our treasure is, there will our heart be also.

Second, we would also learn that we cannot specify what activities are legitimate for others when the issues are not entirely clear. My weakness may not be yours; yours might not be mine. It is conceivable that something which leads me astray might not have a similar effect on you. We would each have to determine before God and the Scriptures what He wanted *us* to do. We would not be critical of others who do not fit into our prescribed pattern. When we did see faults in others, we would help them in love rather than with self-righteous condemnation.

Finally, something else equally important would happen: we would begin to see the utter impossibility of living the Christian life. God's desire for inward purity would loom so great that we would be driven to Him for supernatural ability. We would see that He demands so much that only He can supply what He demands!

The standards we had formerly followed would suddenly shrivel in comparison to His stringent demands. Petty distinctions would pale in comparison to the weightier matters of honesty, purity, and the fruit of the Spirit. We would feel helpless, morally weak, and wholly inadequate. And this would be the beginning of a totally different perspective of Christianity; a perspective that would once again make God a necessity for living a Christian life.

This perspective will help us realize that those who live in the power of the Holy Spirit have not been gypped. Christ has not trapped us into being good while others can have a good time. His restrictions were given to show us more keenly our need of Him. Once we have seen this dimension of the Christian life, we would no longer believe Satan's lie, namely, that Christ came to take the fun out of life.

We would understand that a Christian is more than a sinner minus his sins; never again would we settle for living according to a pattern of behavior by sheer willpower. There would be a supernatural aspect to our lives defying human explanation. And perhaps for the first time, we would understand what Christ meant when He said that He came to give us *life* and to give it more abundantly.

Then if we were arrested for being a Christian, there would finally be enough evidence to convict us. Our lifestyle would demonstrate that we are living in dependence on the living God. *That* is the first prerequisite for genuine Christian conduct!

8

HOW DOLLARS CAN MAKE SENSE

MONEY DOES TALK. Listen carefully to what it says:

> Dug from the mountain side
>   Or washed in the glen,
>   Servant am I or master of men.
> Earn me, I bless you;
> Steal me, I curse you;
>   Grasp me and hold me,
> A fiend shall possess you.
>   Lie for me, die for me,
>   Covet me, take me—
> Angel or devil,
>   I'm just what you make me.
>
>   AUTHOR UNKNOWN

Everything God has given us is a test of our loyalty. But our attitude toward money is an especially accurate barometer of our relationship to the world. In fact, no man who loves money can simultaneously love God. John wrote, "But whoever has the world's goods, and beholds his brother in need and closes his heart against him, how does the love of God abide in him?" (1 Jn 3:17). To love money is to hate God.

Often the subject of money is misunderstood or ignored. Sometimes, believers become weary of hearing about stewardship, or they misunderstand what the Scriptures teach concerning their paycheck. As a result, their spiritual development is stifled.

One of the most common misconceptions buried deeply in the minds of many is that stewardship (using our money for God) is a good idea—for the rich. Consequently we excuse ourselves. We are convinced that if we had a million dollars we would give God half of it. But the truth is, we wouldn't—unless we are giving a generous proportion *now*. Perhaps only a mental volcano can pry us loose from the notion that we should not bother trying to understand the scriptural principles of giving and buying because we do not have much to spend or give. Such reasoning has two deceptions. First, it assumes that God considers giving from a utilitarian viewpoint (how much actual good our money does), rather than from a spiritual standpoint (the attitude in which it was given). From the standpoint of *results,* the widow who gave two mites accomplished nothing. How much gold did her two cents buy to complete the Temple decorations? How many priests were able to buy a meal with what she put in? None. But Jesus said that she gave more than those who put in enough money to *do* something, such as to finish the Temple, to pay the priests, and hopefully to help the poor.

Fifty dollars will buy a missionary some equipment. Twenty will help pay the utility bills of the church. One dollar buys a few stamps. Two pennies? *Spare the effort of putting them into the offering plate. Give when you can make it worthwhile so that something can be done with the amount.* Does such reasoning sound familiar? This philosophy lurks in the back of many minds, like the Pharisees who thought that God wanted money— lots of it—so that something worthwhile could be accomplished on earth. But Jesus said that the two cents were worth more in God's book than fifty dollars. With that philosophy of arithmetic, a certified accountant would lose his job in a day.

But God doesn't count money by adding it together or by calculating how much it will buy. Those who give much without sacrifice are reckoned as having given little; those who give from all their living are reckoned as having given much. Without that basic understanding, we've missed the purpose of giving—and we've missed it by a mile.

The second deception in this philosophy is that we are poor while others are rich. Certainly some do have more than we, and these people look to others who have more than they, and so it goes ad nauseum. But we forget that millions have less than any of us. In many countries of the world, it would take a day to earn enough money to buy this book. In some places of the world, naked children lick crumbs of bread and decayed meat that have fallen onto the streets. For them, anyone who can afford a pair of shoes is wealthy. We have become so tainted by the affluence of our day that we have lost sight of what God has given us. Many of us have never had to pray, "Give us our daily bread." We spend more time counting our calories than we do our blessings.

One of the most accurate barometers of our spiritual maturity is the way we use our money. In the Scriptures, a wrong attitude toward money is directly associated with worldliness and godlessness. Think of the money in your pocket right now. Two dollars? Two cents? How you spend it may reflect whether you are in the world though not of it. If we use it properly, we will not lose it; if we misuse it, it will be snatched from us. Like the rich fool, we will have gained the whole world (or tried to) but will have lost our own soul.

The most basic truth that God wants to teach us regarding our money is that *all* of it belongs to Him. Whenever we use it selfishly, we rob God, since it rightfully belongs to Him. The first step in becoming detached from the love of money is to recognize that everything we have is His, and, therefore, we must consciously return our bank accounts to God. This will rid us of the notion that we can give God His portion on Sunday and, having fulfilled our duty, spend the rest on ourselves. Many of us Christians still have two separate compartments in our minds. God gets His share, perhaps ten percent or less, and we get the rest. God gets one part, and we get nine. God can use His part as He wishes, and we can use our part as we wish. What more can God ask, especially with rising inflation? Answer: He asks for it all.

Obviously we should give a part of our money to the church, missionaries, and other worthy causes. But let us remember that God will not merely judge us on the basis of what we gave but also on the basis of what we did with what we kept for ourselves. That too belongs to Him. We will be accountable for every dollar we have earned.

How then should we handle God's money? For one thing, it means learning to depend on God for wisdom to use it in the best possible way. Certainly God may want us to have a new vacuum cleaner, car, or suit of clothes. But since we are buying these items with God's money, they in turn also belong to Him. What we spend on ourselves is just as much God's as what we put into the offering plate.

Look at it this way. If your employer gave you a hundred-dollar bill and asked you to spend it wisely and give an account to him for it, you would spend it very carefully. At the end of the day you would give him an itemized list of what you had bought, and you would be prepared to justify every expenditure. But if that one hundred-dollar bill was yours, you could squander it or even lose it without having to answer for your actions.

When we realize that our money is lent to us by God, we will be careful how we spend it. As we see others who are in need, we will learn to distinguish between our own needs (the basic necessities) and our wants. God may permit us to have some luxuries and to spend His money for our enjoyment, but we will not insist on such privileges. Having food and clothing, we will be content.

The advertising industry has created the impression that luxuries are necessities and wants are needs. We can enjoy whatever we like now and pay later. This desire for things has become so powerful that Christians have also become the victims of endless monthly payments and high interest rates. Credit cards make it almost impossible to bypass a bargain. Eventually we are drowned in a swamp of debts. What is the answer?

Part of the solution is to recognize that since our money belongs to God, we have no right to covet the conveniences and luxuries others might have. To borrow money for a wise investment may be necessary; but to go into debt for a luxury is foolishness. We should realize that God may deprive us of certain wants—as well as necessities—in order to teach us to trust Him. Too often our credit card becomes a substitute for our heavenly Father who knows in advance what we need. The first principle of finances is, consciously give all that you have to God and depend on Him for wisdom on how to spend what He has lent you, whether that is little or much.

Christ taught another financial principle by means of a parable. An unjust steward used the possessions of his master to make friends so that when he was fired, he could depend on these friends to accept him into their home (Lk 16:1-13). Christ taught that we should use money to make friendships that have lasting value, but even more important, He added, "He who is faithful in a very little thing is faithful also in much; and he who is unrighteous in a very little thing is unrighteous also in much" (16:10). Money is the real test of a man's character. This is why God is not so concerned whether we have little or whether we have much; He tells us that our attitude will be the basis of His evaluation. If we are faithful with two dollars, we will be faithful with two hundred. If we are unfaithful with one dollar, God knows that we will be unfaithful with two.

In another parable, Christ taught the same principle even more forcibly. A worthless slave had all of his money taken away from him because he didn't use his master's money wisely (Lk 19:12-26). The servants who invested their master's money profitably were given authority over a proportionate number of cities. But the servant who hid his master's money without investing it had his money snatched from him and given to another. Christ's point is clear: in God's Kingdom, we will be given responsibility only to the extent that we were faithful with God's money on earth. Treasures in heaven are accumulated by our attitude to our treasures (or lack of them) on earth.

Sometimes we associate heavenly rewards with winning people to Christ, teaching Sunday school, or memorizing Scripture. And if we have done these things in dependence upon Christ, we shall not lose our reward. But how many of us believe that our heavenly riches will be directly related to the way in which we invested our nickels, dimes, and dollars on earth? This jingle by an unknown poet puts it accurately:

> It's not what you'd do with a million
> If riches should be your lot
> It's what you are doing at present
> With the dollar and quarter you've got.

We're tempted to ask, But why does God choose money as the test of our loyalty to Him? Why not faithfulness in Sunday school or using our other "talents"? Certainly these related gifts enter into the total picture of God's evaluation of us. But money is emphasized in Scripture simply because our temptation to love it is inexplicably powerful. The fact is that few people have the spiritual resources needed to be both wealthy and godly. As Christ vividly explained, it is easier for a camel to go through the eye of a needle than for a rich man to enter the Kingdom of God.

Paul wrote, "But those who want to get rich fall into temptation and a snare and many foolish and harmful desires which plunge men into ruin and destruction" '(1 Ti 6:9). A Christian man who works at a prominent bank in downtown Chicago and is responsible for counting millions of dollars, stated that employees were constantly being fired for theft, even though they knew that they were being checked for honesty. The temptation was too great, even though being caught was inevitable.

Money is only one part of a man's life, but the love of it is the root of all sorts of evil (1 Ti 6:10). Many Christians are unaware of how deceitful wealth (or the lack of it) can be. Under the guise of having to "earn a living," all sorts of selfishness is tolerated. The rich are vulnerable to sin because they are tempted to have more; those who have little are determined to cling selfishly to what they already have. The legitimate need to earn a living turns out to be the central motivation in some lives where God is consulted only in the case of emergencies.

Most warnings in Scripture are directed to all men, rich or poor. The basic problem is not wealth or lack of it but rather the human heart. The rich may face unique problems because of their desire to get more; but the poor face the same temptations in their desire to get rich. So, in God's eyes, the rich as well as the poor are tested by their attitude toward what they have as well as toward what they would like to have. Money talks. It speaks either the language of the world or the language of God.

Let us suppose that we knew in advance that a certain company would go bankrupt within a short time. We would never invest our money in such a risky venture. We would choose a reliable bank with guaranteed interest. Yet, whenever we use our money as though it is our own, whenever we spend it for the things we want without any consideration of its rightful Owner, we have invested it in the system of this world, a stock market that has already collapsed. Our bankruptcy is as inevitable as the sunrise.

In Christ's day, there were three primary sources of wealth: clothes, grain, and gold. Christ predicted that moths would eat the clothes, rust (blight and rot) would eat the grain, and thieves would steal the gold. Even thought our wealth today might be more secure, the Scriptures teach that we have brought nothing into this world and it is equally certain that we will carry nothing out. To invest our money in the world is to have lived in vain. One day when Alexander the Great was looking dejected, one of his generals said to him, "You have conquered the world; what more can you ask? To which Alexander replied, "You are right, but what I have will not last!"

The alternative is to invest our money in the bank of heaven which is not affected by the variable trends of the Dow Jones Industrial Average. We can spend our money in such a way that the dividends will not even be affected by inflation. God has ordained that we should give money toward the needs of others to display our love and to weld us together more closely in the work He has given us here on earth. Let us consider more specifically what this involves.

GIVING

Preacher to Farmer: If you had two farms, would you give one of them to God?

Farmer: Of course, you know I would!

Preacher: If you had two thousand dollars, would you give one thousand to God?

Farmer: Why certainly I would!

Preacher: If you had two pigs—

Farmer: Now preacher, that's not fair, you know I have two pigs.

The subject of giving often makes Christians a bit

uneasy, or else it puts them to sleep. We have been so bombarded with letters, offerings, and solicitations that we cannot sort them out. Since most of us find it easier to spend money than to give it, we prefer to be immune to the constant pleas for needed funds here and help with deficits there. Someone has suggested that it is time for a moratorium on giving.

Maybe it is. At least we should pause long enough to find out what the Bible teaches on the subject. And in the process, we might be awakened to realize that God has some pointed suggestions about how we should use what He has given us.

Today there are a host of worthy chuches and organizations that need funds. In desperation, some of them have hired teams of experts to analyze their constituency and evaluate the financial assets of a given community. The experts' job description is clear: extract the needed funds from the constituency, using any method (or almost any method) that will work. Then promote the program as "honoring to God," since this money will be used to prop up His interests in the world. Letters containing direct appeals for money (even a minimum amount expected) are accompanied by a visit from the appointed fund raiser. One man, hired to raise a few million dollars for one Christian organization, passed this tip to local pastors. "We've found that people give more when they fill out their pledges in the presence of someone else." Undoubtedly, they do. At least Ananias and Sapphira did.

While I have been writing this, two brochures have come to my desk with information on how to raise money for churches, schools, and civic organizations. The methods have been proven and are guaranteed to succeed. One brochure boasts that with proper techniques, almost any church can practically double its church budget. Trained fund raisers know in advance that their methods achieve the desired results.

We should not dispute their claims. It is true that churches can increase their budget, mission boards can operate in the black, and Christian schools can pay their faculty members by using hard sell and direct appeals. Nor do we suggest that such organizations are unworthy of proper financial support. Hundreds of evangelical churches and organizations are dedicated to proclaim the Gospel. Many of these are dependent upon the gifts of the Christian community. But should we succumb to the financial burdens and use modern techniques to pressure Christians into sharing their wealth? Or might it be that a lack of funds should be handled in other ways? In short, what does the Bible have to say about giving?

Since most Christians immediately think of tithing when money or stewardship is mentioned, perhaps the first question that should be asked is whether tithing is a requirement for the New Testament church. The answer is no. The word *tithe* is found eight times in the New Testament. In the gospels it is used with reference to the Pharisees who were tithing only to fulfill their obligations to the Mosaic law (Mt 23:23; Lk 11:42; 18:12). The only other occurrences of the word are in Hebrews 7, where the priesthood of Melchizedek is shown to be superior to that of Levi. If tithing were a requirement, we would expect that such a commandment would appear in the New Testament. Several chapters are devoted to the subject of giving in the New Testament; yet tithing is not mentioned.

112

The tithe was a part of the Mosaic law, which was never given to Gentiles and which has been done away in Christ (2 Co 3:7-13). Even the oft quoted words of Malachi 3 are expressly addressed to the sons of Jacob. To the Jews, God promised material prosperity if they would bring tithes and offerings and make proper use of their land. But today, prosperity is not necessarily a sign of godly living, and godly living does not guarantee prosperity. Those who have not seen the basic difference between God's dealings with the nation Israel and His relationship to the Church have falsely concluded that God is obligated to bless us materially if we give a certain percentage of our income to Him. One book entitled *How to Give Your Way to Prosperity* suggests that we can, if we wish, become wealthy by giving. This was true for the nation Israel, living in the land God had provided, but no such promises are made in the New Testament for the Church in this age.

Furthermore, in the Old Testament, tithing was a form of taxation imposed on all the Israelites. In fact, there were at least three tithes. One was for the maintenance of the Levites, since they were responsible for the work of the tabernacle (Lev 27:30-33). There was also the tithe for the national feasts and sacrifices (Deu 12:5-6; 14:22-24), and finally there was a tithe every third year used for the poor of the land (Deu 14:28-29). This means that an Israelite might be expected to give more than twenty percent of his income to support the various observances God commanded. This was mandatory. Over and above this, he was to bring his gifts as a freewill offering to God (Mal 3:8-10). As far as *giving* is concerned, there is no amount specified by God, either in the Old Testament or the New.

113

Many Christian leaders admit privately that tithing is not a New Testament requirement but justify an emphasis on tithing by saying that since God demanded ten percent under the Law, it is not asking too much to require that much or more under grace. Such reasoning is based on the fear that if tithing is not taught as a requirement, then Christians might end up giving nothing at all. So to insure the fact that some money will flow into the depleted coffers, tithing is taught despite the fact that it lacks scriptural support. Such reasoning has two flaws. One is that when people give for a wrong motive, such offerings are unacceptable to God. This can be shown by the frequent references in the Old Testament to God's loathing the offerings of His people (Is 1:12-15). The second error is that we fail to see that if believers give with a proper motivation, they will gladly give beyond ten percent. Therefore, in the long run, an emphasis on tithing hinders rather than increases the amount of money given.

Detailed instructions on giving are found in 2 Corinthians 8 and 9. Paul begins his discussion by using the Christians of Macedonia as an example of giving that is acceptable to God. The Macedonians were devastated by an earthquake and had gone through a series of tragedies. Yet they gave extensively out of their poverty to the needy saints at Jerusalem (2 Co 8:1-6). Paul says that they did not merely give according to their ability but even *beyond* their ability. No one had demanded anything of them. There was no requirement they were expected to meet. In fact, they *begged* for the opportunity to participate in the support of other saints (vv. 3-4). In our day, such an attitude is so rare that, if we found a church that would plead for the privilege

114

of giving to the need of others, we would consider the members odd if not fanatical. What could be the secret of their generosity?

Paul writes, "They first gave themselves to the Lord" (v. 5). Perhaps the reason they were a model church in giving is that they were a model church in dedication. If Paul had taught tithing as a requirement, he would have dampened their motivation. Or at least such teaching would have obscured the true purpose of why they wanted to give. But there was no reason to require something of them. They gave without any compulsion beyond what was humanly expected.

The Macedonians' enthusiasm for helping the needy was not shared by the Corinthians. An offering had been started among them, but it had not been completed. Titus was being sent back to them, and Paul wanted to encourage the Corinthians to give with the right motivation. He stated clearly that he is not demanding that they give (v. 8), for this would be inconsistent with the kind of motivation God accepts. Paul wanted them to be motivated by the example of Christ, who, "though He was rich, yet for your sake He became poor, that you through His poverty might become rich" (v. 9). The most basic principle of giving is that we should give because Christ gave; we should not give because we must nor because we have to meet our budget, but because we want to express our love for Christ by our gifts. Christ is our example.

Let's take a closer look at a few of the principles of giving. Paul writes, "Let each one do just as he has purposed in his heart; not grudgingly or under compulsion; for God loves a cheerful giver" (2 Co 9:7). First, we are not to give with a stingy attitude. Money given with resentment does not honor God. It might help meet the budget, but this does not justify the gift. Since God has given to us so generously, it is an insult to give to Him grudgingly. Consequently, it is better not to give at all than to regret the fact that we have to part with such hard-earned cash. Some Christians think of giving as one of those painful experiences we must endure if we want to receive the benefits of the church. With such an attiude, it is better to look straight ahead and let the offering plate pass by.

Just to emphasize how important our attitude is, Paul says that if our hearts are right, we are acceptable to God even when we cannot give anything. "If you are really eager to give, then it isn't important how much you have to give. God wants you to give what you have, not what you haven't" (2 Co 8:12, TLB). As mentioned earlier, God is more concerned with our mental attitude than He is with the amount we give. That is why the widow who gave two mites gave more than those who paid for the gold furnishings in the Temple.

Second, Paul says we should not give out the compulsion. We should not give because we feel forced to give. Giving is not something that can be imposed upon us by a fund-raising committee that reaches its objectives by having someone else present when the pledges are being signed. Any gimmicks that trap people into giving are to be abhorred.

It follows that giving should therefore be a private matter between each individual and God. In 1 Corinthians 16:2, Paul emphasized that each one should put aside and save some money for the church. In the Greek, a reflexive pronoun translated literally "to himself," indicates that the gift was to be kept in a private deposit.

Out of this, the believer should distribute to specific causes, as well as give to the ministry of the church on the first day of the week.

Whenever one's giving becomes public knowledge, there is the temptation to judge others, to make unfavorable comparisons (as well as favorable ones), and we are forced to give out of compulsion. Like the Pharisees who gave to be noticed, there is the danger that the privilege of giving will degenerate into a carnal duty.

A third principle is that we should give proportionately. In 1 Corinthians 16:2, Paul writes that each should give as God has prospered him. Understandably, those who have much will be able to give a greater amount than those who have little. There is nothing wrong with deciding that a certain percentage of our income should be given to the Lord's work in the church or other evangelical causes.

Since no percentage is stipulated, it could be ten, fifteen, or fifty percent. Or even more. To choose ten percent is not wrong, just as long as it is not done dutifully as a required "tithe." In other words, many who do tithe do not do so legalistically; they do not give out of necessity or grudgingly. But we err when we choose a certain percentage and maintain that fraction year after year without any further consideration.

Paul seems to imply that on the Lord's Day, we ought to decide how much to lay aside for that week. Many believers simply give a certain amount on Sunday and never stop to evaluate what they should do in a specific situation. They have fallen into such a rut that they never even think about consulting the Lord to find out what He might want them to give. This does not mean that we should give spasmodically or just according to any impulse we might have. It does mean that we should be sensitive to the proportion we give, being ready to increase it as the Lord enables us to. Churches often discover that their income remains the same year after year, even though the members' standard of living has been rising. While increases come in salary, there are often no increases in giving. The solution is not to hire a team of experts to collect the needed funds; rather we must see stinginess as carnality displayed in a concrete form. Unless we move insensitive believers to spiritual maturity, we have not done anything worthy of eternal reward, even if we reach our budget by clever programs.

Then what should churches do when the needed money is not available? What should missionary societies do when they do not have enough to send out missionaries? Do these needs justify some coercion? A dollar given grudgingly might mean the giver will lose his reward, but it will help get the Gospel to the ends of the earth. At least that is the way we are tempted to reason.

Let us remember that it is legitimate to make needs known. Some godly men of the past have not even shared the needs of their work with others but have shared them with God alone. God honored their faith, and often their needs were met miraculously. However, the apostle Paul spoke openly about the needs of the saints at Jerusalem. In order to give intelligently, it is necessary to know what is needed, where the gift is going and what it is intended to accomplish. Needs can be made known. And we might add that the laborer is worthy of his hire. It is a shame for a spiritual leader to live in poverty while his constituency lives in wealth.

Beyond this, however, we cannot legitimately go. We cannot demand a certain sum because of a deficit. After

118

the needs have been exposed, we have to face a question: is this work (church, mission board, outreach, etc.) of God? If it is our own work, we had better get money from somewhere; if the work is God's, it is *His* responsibility to put it upon the hearts of His children to help meet the need.

These last few paragraphs do not mean that we should be unconcerned if churches and worthy Christian organizations collapse for lack of funds. When this happens, it is a sad commentary on our day. Even wealthy Christians are often miserly in their support of the church. But my plea is, rather than letting the shortage of funds drive us to promotional gimmicks that would go beyond scriptural principles, let the shortage of funds drive us to our knees for our church, missionary programs, and country. God is trying to tell us something through the many existing needs, but let us not respond in the wrong way. Let us repent of our carnality, seek His face, and depend on Him alone. He will honor such faith.

9

TWENTIETH-CENTURY FIG LEAVES

Do you dress like a Christian? Perhaps the question should be even more basic: should Christians dress differently than society? Do clothes have anything to do with worldliness?

Ever since Adam and Eve sewed fig leaves together, clothing has been a part of our heritage. Presumably, if they had not sinned, clothing would not have become a necessity, except as protection from the elements. But after Adam and Eve sinned, they tried to hide their guilt by cowering in the bushes; they also tried to cover their shame by wearing aprons.

Now that sin was in the world, God approved of Adam and Eve's desire for clothing. The Almighty exchanged their fig leaves for coats made of skins. From then on, clothes were needed not only to cover the shame of bodies affected by sin but also as an aid to preserving moral purity. Modesty had then become necessary in our fallen world.

Of course, wearing clothes does not insure modesty. Clothing worn to appeal to the imagination may be more seductive than the accepted seminudity of some remote cultures.

This, however, does not mean that we should be indifferent to current pressures toward making public

120

nudity acceptable. In American culture, such trends are directly related to sexual permissiveness and sensuality. Some mistakenly assume that rejecting the inhibitions of the past is the path to true freedom, but the effects of sin cannot be ignored easily. Shedding clothes can neither obliterate guilt nor can it erase shame. Those who seek freedom by permissiveness are led further into moral bondage.

A discussion of clothing is not merely a discussion of cultural acceptance. For the Christain, it is also a discussion of what the Bible teaches about clothing and our attitude toward it.

In the Old Testament, God gave a command, "A woman shall not wear man's clothing, nor shall a man put on a woman's clothing; for whoever does these things is an abomination to the LORD your God" (Deu 22:5). This does not mean that a woman should never wear slacks. Some occasions call for them. This command was directed to the Israelites, along with hundreds of other detailed laws, for the purpose of preserving the peculiarity of the sexes. Every invasion of the natural distinctions between men and women violates God's order. This command prohibits transvestism (the adoption of the dress and behavior of the opposite sex).

In our day, unisex clothing stores are becoming popular. Barber shops also advertise unisex haircuts which blur the natural distinctions between the sexes (1 Co 11:14-15). Since clothing itself is morally neutral and since hair styles are directly related to cultural acceptance, it would be easy to conclude that unisex trends have no great moral significance. But they do. Disregarding the distinctions between men and women is

121

symptomatic of moral deviation. Although both sexes are equal, they also have distinct functions and roles.

Clothes and hairstyles can communicate identity. Several years ago, when the hippie movement began, the unofficial sign of membership for males was shoulder-length hair. Then, as longer hairstyles were more widely accepted, the length of hair no longer conveyed the same meaning. Similarly, certain types of clothing are often worn to identify with a given culture or subculture.

Deuteronomy 22:5 reminds us of an important principle: the clothes we wear often reflect our inner attitudes. Clothes often are used to call attention to what we feel within. Clothes can communicate a message.

Consider the young person who wears patched blue jeans to church. He may have other clothes at home but prefers to show up with the most worn pair he can find. By rejecting the accepted Sunday attire, he calls attention to himself and is silently asking, "Do you accept me for who I am or for the clothes I wear?" If he is asked to sit in the back row—if indeed he is permitted to sit at all—he has received the answer he suspected was coming, namely, that he is unwelcome in his casual garb.

Arguments over such matters only compound the problem. The Church must be willing to love all people, even those who dress to get attention. Such people are crying for acceptance, and it is our duty—our privilege—to accept them as Christ accepts us.

Clothes communicate attitudes. We can communicate by dressing poorly, extravagantly, or immodestly. In any apparel we wear, we may be reflecting our attitude to society around us.

In chapter two, we saw that a primary characteristic of worldliness is putting the wrong value on legitimate concerns. Clothing is necessary. But we can become a slave to new styles and fashions. Christ taught that anxiety about clothing was characteristic of worldly attitudes (Mt 6:25).

In our day, this anxiety is expressed by a perpetual desire to be in style. Whether or not we realize it, we wear what the fashion designers decide we will wear.

The mass media has made us self-conscious. Woe unto those who are not squeezed into the mold! Clothing that looked so right five years ago looks so wrong today.

Harvey Cox, in *The Secular City,* scrutinizes the insecurity of our age. Changes take place so rapidly that no one can keep up with them. The insecure and anxious constantly read the latest magazines, look at the latest ads, and admire the latest public hero. According to Cox, this is one of the reasons for the success of *Playboy* magazine. The reader, Cox says, knows that "the style will change and he must always be ready to adjust. His persistent anxiety that he may mix a drink incorrectly, enjoy a jazz group that is passe or wear last year's necktie style is comforted by an authoritative tone in *Playboy* beside which papal encyclicals sound irresolute."[1]

Cox continues, "Those liberated by technology and increased prosperity to new worlds of leisure now become the anxious slaves of dictatorial tastemakers. . . . *Playboy* mediates the Word of the most high into one

---

1. Harvey Cox, *The Secular City,* rev. ed. (New York: Macmillan, 1966), p. 175.

section of the consumer world, but it is a word of bondage, not of freedom."[2]

All of us can succumb to the anxiety for the latest styles. Clothes can be used to protect our facade. Some men go to church to display the suits that they could not conveniently wear during the week. Women have been known to skip a banquet or reject a wedding invitation because "I have nothing to wear," which, more accurately stated, is, "I have nothing *new* to wear." Unfortunately, attending church often means little more than joining the fashion parade.

In their constant quest for new fads, designers often resurrect the styles of twenty years ago. Since styles are based purely on conventional acceptance, Spurgeon aptly defined fashion as "the collective opinion of fools."

Of course, new styles are not sinful. Neither is there anything inherently spiritual about adopting styles five years late. But anxiety about whether we are wearing the latest fashions indicates that our security is misplaced.

There is no virtue in old fashions, but apart from social acceptance there is no virtue in the new ones either. We can influence our friends by the way we dress, but God remains unimpressed.

Since styles vary from culture to culture and era to era, should Christians have standards in matters of dress? Do schools have a right to demand dress codes? If so, how can lines be drawn?

DRAWING THAT INVISIBLE LINE

In a logic class in the university, our instructor ex-

2. Ibid., p. 176.

plained six logical fallacies. One was entitled, "The Argument of the Beard." Briefly, our assignment was to decide how many hairs constitute a beard. Two? Hardly. Fifty? It's doubtful. Four hundred? Perhaps. But what about 399 or 398? How do you know when you have crossed the line? Answer: You don't. Obviously, there is no way to settle the question as to how many hairs are needed to make a beard. Someone else could always suggest one more or one less. And there would be no way to prove which arbitrary choice is right.

Now let us suppose that the president of a company insisted that his manager hire only men with beards. Could the manager carry out such instructions? Or would the manager have to say, "Since we have no authoritative way to distinguish between someone who has a beard and one who does not, we cannot grant the president's request"? Sound a bit silly?

If we follow this reasoning to its logical conclusion, it leads to absurdity. We would end up being unwilling to classify anyone as either having a beard or not having one, simply because we do not know where to draw the line. But obviously there is a great difference between a few whiskers and a beard; there is even a significant difference between someone with a full beard and someone with a goatee, even though we can not decide precisely when one becomes the other.

The point that the professor was trying to make is that although there is no exact way to distinguish between someone who has a beard and someone who does not, it is wrong to assume that we cannot recognize significant differences between them. To put it another way, important differences may exist between two quite similar entities, even though we cannot easily pinpoint where

125

they differ. We must draw lines even where fine distinctions are involved, even when our lines have to be quite arbitrary. It is simply not true that we should consider two things as equal because a distinction between them may be difficult to make.

This is why censorship usually fails in our free society. One group of judges may decide to draw the line at one point; others may choose another. But no one can say authoritatively where art ends and pornography begins. Can it be defined in terms of the amount of clothes or lack of them worn by the model? Why is one pose suggestive and another not? Add to this the fact that one picture affects each individual differently (depending on his background, taboos, or life-style), and any distinctions whatever dissolve into an undifferentiated blur. Consequently, pornography peddlers insist that all types of books and movies should be permissible simply because no one can define pornography with precision. So in the absence of authoritative guidelines, our society is beginning to accept all types of reading and viewing material without raising an eyebrow.

Such reasoning is ridiculous. Just as a great difference exists between a full beard and a half-dozen whiskers, a vast difference exists between pornography and *Time* magazine. There is also a difference between one suggestive scene and an X-rated movie. It still remains necessary to decide what is pornography and what is not, what is decent and what is indecent, even in situations where the issues are not altogether clear. And usually, it is much easier to draw the line than some of our modern hedonists would like us to believe. There may be some differences of opinion, but that does not mean we are justified in accepting all types of art, movies, and literature. Briefly, the difficulty with making fine distinctions should not lead us to believe that everything can be classified as being on the same level. We must be willing to draw lines personally and corporately.[3]

The same principle applies to making other types of rules as well. Parents are constantly faced with the decision of making rules for their children; Christian schools often revise their handbooks. Questions arise regarding hairstyles, dress codes, and personal conduct. Sometimes making such rules necessitates arbitrary distinctions. Yet such distinctions must be made.

Imagine a continuum between one and a hundred. Suppose the number one represents an extremely strict, rigid life-style. Let the number one hundred represent permissive and irresponsible conduct. All of the other numbers represent varying types of life-styles, progressing steadily from the most strict (number one) to the most permissive (number one hundred). Now imagine that parents decide to give their children freedom up to the number 30. Admittedly, the choice is arbitrary, since there is no great difference between thirty and thirty-one. But they have to draw the line somewhere. Perhaps next year they will tighten the requirements, choosing number twenty-five; or they may become more lenient and choose number thirty-five. Just because there may be latitude for change—even disagreement—does not mean that parents and schools should permit all

---

3. State Senator John Harmer of California circulated a petition against pornography, stating specifically how he believed obscenity should be defined. Although his description was violently opposed by the publishers of pornography, he provides an excellent example of how a line must be drawn somewhere— even if arbitrarily—in order to prevent immoral influences (*Time,* October 23, 1972, p. 36).

styles of conduct because they cannot decide with absolute certainty where to draw the line.

Decide they must! For if they do not make a stopping point somewhere on the continuum, some people would choose level of conduct number one hundred and be ruined in the process.

Can we draw the line in matters where the issues are not entirely clear? Yes. We cannot allow the difficulty of making precise distinctions frighten us into making no distinctions at all! We need the wisdom of God in knowing how to strike a balance between severe restrictions, that would deny believers legitimate pleasures, and an atmosphere of leniency, that would permit all types of conduct under the guise of Christian liberty.

Suitable Modesty

Let's apply this principle to the question of modest clothing. A designer of enticing women's apparel candidly remarked that fashions were purposely abbreviated "because a woman should be just as seductive in the daytime as she is at night." Swimsuits have been trimmed to the least possible coverage in order to accentuate sexual attraction. Those who wear less appealing clothes are labeled prudes.

Making distinctions in our permissive society is not easy. For example, at what point does a skirt become a a miniskirt? Four inches above the knee? Three and a half? Such questions are technically unanswerable. There is no point measurable in inches and centimeters where modesty ends and immodesty begins. And for this reason, many have falsely concluded that it doesn't matter what they wear. Since no precise limits can be agreed upon, all forms of dress have been assumed to be on the same level. But they aren't!

Once again, while we may admit that no one can measure modesty with a yardstick, it may be necessary to choose a measurable requirement and adhere to it. Those who make such decisions are frequently accused of being arbitrary and of making petty distinctions. Certainly such a charge is sometimes justified, especially in matters where no biblical principle is involved. But in many instances fine distinctions are necessary. In fact, there are times when a rule can only be made arbitrarily. We must choose a certain point beyond which we—and those for whom we are responsible—cannot go.

Obviously there will be disagreements as to where lines should be drawn on specific issues. There will be differences from country to country and family to family. For example, modest apparel in the Far East may indeed be different from modest apparel in the United States. Also the modesty of previous centuries (where elbows and ankles had to be covered) may not be the modesty of today. Usually when new forms of dress are introduced into a culture, they may be thought immodest until they are not given a second thought or glance. This explains why Christians may shun certain styles at first and then accept them in the next generation. Such changes do not reflect unfavorably on the preceding generation, since standards of acceptance vary. Nor should we pride ourselves in being enlightened because we think we have overcome some of the hang-ups of the past. Remember that God's standards have not changed, even though we may have adopted new styles or changed some of our rules. Once again, we must be driven back to principles of purity, honesty, and consideration for others, which transcend all cultural gaps. We will have differences—choosing different points along the continuum—but we should avoid petty scruples. We should especially be careful to avoid dogmatism in matters where no moral issues are at stake.

Remember also that we must not exercise our freedom if it would hinder others in the Christian life. We should be willing to lay aside weights which might not only be a burden to us but to others as well. Let's not be quick to judge others who have drawn the line at a different point than we would. We may have weaknesses they do not have; conversely, they may need restrictions we find unnecessary. Of course, we should understand that such flexibility applies only to areas where the moral and spiritual implications are unclear, and, therefore, legitimate differences exist.

Cultural Acceptance

What about instances where dress codes have nothing to do with modesty or immodesty but are purely matters of cultural acceptance? For example, here is a quotation from a Christian school's handbook: "Young men will wear shirts and ties to all classes and coats to the noon and evening meals. The student body will always dress appropriately and will adhere to standards that will please fundamental Christian parents across America."

Obviously sports coats and ties have nothing to do with modesty. Such restrictions have no scriptural basis whatever. Does this mean that such rules are unnecessary, irrelevant, or evil? Such standards are legitimate, as long as the faculty and students understand clearly

130

that such conformity is not the result of any biblical principle but rather the result of social pressure from the evangelical (fundamental) community. These requirements are made for sociological reasons (pleasing the parents, status in the community, getting jobs, or being acceptable to certain churches). Such requirements are proper for the above reasons, but this should be clarified, lest such rules are considered synonymous with Christianity.

Many parents have discovered to their dismay that children can easily conform to the dress codes (and standards) of the church and yet reject their heritage when they come of age. Unfortunately, part of the reason is that we have evaluated them outwardly and thought all was well because they appeared to conform to mores of the church or school. One of the most subtle pharisaical errors is to cleanse the outside of the cup (everyone probably was required to wear just the right robes) yet inwardly be filthy (Mt 23:25). Christ's remark to them was, "First clean the inside of the cup and of the dish, so that the outside of it may become clean also" (v. 26). To put it in contemporary terms: Whenever we dress in our best clothes (suits and ties on Sunday), we had better know that this in no way means that we are pleasing to God. The poor who have no suits and see no need for ties and come to church barefoot might well enter the Kingdom of heaven ahead of us.

On the other hand, we should not be critical of those who happen to be in step with the fashions of the day. Parents have often unwisely forced their children to wear clothes of the past generation, thinking that contemporary styles were sinful. This gives the erroneous impression that a Christian is one who is always ten years behind the times.

To be balanced, we should gladly accept new styles which are purely cultural. Yet on the other hand, it is sinful to be obsessed with every present fad. Those who use clothing to enhance their social status have compromised with the world.

In churches and schools, children and students should be reminded that they have an obligation to obey their parents and those in authority over them (Eph 6:1-2; 1 Ti 5:17). So if restrictions are made, they should be obeyed, even when it seems that such rules are unnecessary. Part of the way we learn discipline is to obey those over us in the Lord, even when they may be wrong. And we should not merely obey outwardly but have a corresponding attitude of obedience as well.

In short, it may be necessary to dress according to certain restrictions, even when biblical principles are not at stake. The reason for such rules are, however, purely cultural and are for the purpose of social acceptance.

PERSONAL APPLICATIONS

Daily we are confronted with the need to make personal decisions. Our appearance does reflect in part our relationship with the world. When the apostle Peter was discussing the conduct of women—especially those women whose husbands were not Christians—he said that the husbands would be won by the behavior of the wives. Then he added, "And let not your adornment be external only—braiding the hair, and wearing gold jewelry, and putting on dresses; but let it be the hidden person of the heart, with the imperishable quality of a

132

gentle and quiet spirit, which is precious in the sight of God" (1 Pe 3:3-4).

Although this is addressed to women, the principle here applies to us all: our inner attitude is more important than the beauty of clothes. To be adorned outwardly and yet be sinful inwardly is hypocrisy. Cleansing the outside of the cup but being filthy inside is scarcely a new ploy.

There is a related principle here as well: clothes should not be used to draw attention away from the enduring qualities of godliness. Perhaps this is what Paul had in mind when he wrote, "I want women to adorn themselves with proper clothing, modestly and discreetly, not with braided hair and gold or pearls or costly garments" (1 Ti 2:9).

Those who dress to impress others or to flaunt their physique have capitulated to the attitude of the world.

We've come a long way from fig leaves, but, as yet, we have not escaped the consequences of our sinful environment. The fact that we are a part of our cultural heritage is not in itself a cause for alarm, except when that culture deviates from the standards of Scripture.

There will always be borderline cases; the issues will often be blurred. It is then that we need to know what is right, what is wrong, and how to draw a line between the two. Doing that necessitates God's wisdom. Blessed are they to whom such is given!

10

A ROUGH SKETCH OF THE FINE ARTS

DIVERGENT OPINIONS regarding art and music often produce sparks—sometimes explosions. If we could eavesdrop in the average Christain home or overhear discussions in the average evangelical church, we would soon learn that discussions about art, especially music, usually generate more heat than light. Contemporary art is usually a distance from us, but contemporary music is never far away, sometimes as near as the upstairs bedroom.

Some Christians believe we should be concerned only about heavenly things (matters that will count for eternity) rather than the "trivia" of the fine arts. Paintings are considered worldly because they represent purely human values; music is considered appropriate only to the extent that it accompanies words with a Christian message.

On the other hand, some Christians contend that Evangelicals are culturally illiterate. As a result, a rash of articles and books has been written to correct what is believed to be a glaring deficiency.

Perhaps the problem is not whether there is a place for art and music in the Christian life; rather, the questions are, What type of art and music is distinctly Christian? How much importance should we attach to these forms of expression? Let us apply these questions to art and music separately.

ART

Although the word *art* often has a broad meaning, we shall use it here to refer only to painting and sculpture. Before we proceed, we must settle the basic question of whether there is any place at all for these expressions in the life of a Christian. Many believe representational art is forbidden in Exodus 20:4: "You shall not make for yourself an idol, or any likeness of what is in heaven above or on the earth beneath or in the water under the earth." Since God says that man is forbidden to make a likeness of *anything* in heaven or earth, some conscientious people conclude that sculpture and painting are prohibited.

However, the immediate context provides the clue to the meaning God intended. The next verse reads, "You shall not worship them or serve them; for I, the LORD your God, am a jealous God." The implication is that God forbade making works of art as objects of worship. This is made clear in Leviticus 26:1, where the Lord repeats His original command but again adds that these objects should not be made as idols; works of art should not become a substitute for worshipping the Lord God. This interpretation is confirmed by the elaborate artwork of the wilderness tabernacle.

However, Christians opposed to art point out that the art in the tabernacle was legitimate only because it was directly concerned with the worship of God. They conclude that art has validity only in so far as it aids in worship. But this view is disproved by Solomon's Temple.

Sometimes we forget that Solomon's Temple was also built according to God's specifications (1 Ch 28:11-12, 19), yet it had much artwork simply for the sake of beauty. For example, Solomon's throne was made of ivory and overlaid with finest gold. Six steps led up to the throne; it had a round top and two lions standing beside each of the arms. Furthermore, twelve lions stood down each side of the steps (1 Ki 10:18-20). These works had no practical value; they were made only for the sake of beauty. So it is not true that God commanded artistic beauty only in matters that pertained to worship.

Frank E. Gaebelein believes that the distinction between so-called secular art and religious art is wrong. In his words, "This [distinction] is wrong in principle, because it assumes a gap between sacred and secular truth and thus violates the unity of truth. Truth, though on its highest level incarnate in Christ and expressed in in the Bible, is not confined to religion. All truth is God's."[1] In other words, art for the Christian need not be limited to purely religious subjects.

This does not mean that all works of art are Christian: we shall see that some art is distinctly pagan. My point is that Christian art *can* include representations which have nothing to do directly with the worship of God. Like the people in Solomon's day, we can appreciate beauty for beauty's sake.

Christ appreciated the beauty of nature. He reminded His disciples that God made the flowers of the field so

---

1. Frank E. Gaebelein, "Toward a Biblical View of Aesthetics," *Christianity Today,* August 30, 1968, p. 4.

beautiful that even Solomon in all his glory did not clothe himself like one of them; the grass of the field was arrayed by the Almighty (Mt 6:28-30). The psalmist appreciated God's creation and exuberantly declared, "The heavens are telling of the glory of God; And the firmament is declaring work of His hands" (Ps 19:1).

In short, God has created us with the ability to appreciate beauty. This may be the beauty of nature or the beauty of man's own handiwork. This capacity is a part of our make-up as creatures created in God's image. As in other disciplines, some have developed their appreciation for beauty more than others. Furthermore, we often grow in our appreciation through study, perception, and concentration. Ben Johnson correctly observed, "Art hath an enemy called ignorance."

Apart from beauty, art often has another function, namely, to communicate a message. Often artists use this vehicle to express their world view. With only slight exaggeration, Marcel Proust wrote, "Only through art can we get outside of ourselves and know another's view of the universe which is not the same as ours and see landscapes which would otherwise have remained unknown to us."[2]

While touring East Germany, I visited the home of Johann Goethe, who lived from 1749-1832. This brilliant writer had made each room reflect his basic humanistic view, which, stated simply, was: man is innately good and, therefore, redeems himself through his noble mind and character. The paintings, sculptures, and even the architecture of the house pointed to the centrality of man. I left Goethe's house with a fresh understanding

---

2. As quoted in John Bartlett, *Familiar Quotations* (Boston: Little, Brown, 1968), p. 908.

of his humanistic philosophy. Art can communicate a message by giving insight into the artist's view of reality.

Obviously, art can be used to communicate a non-Christian world view. I could ·admire Goethe's ability, but I had to reject his philosophy. Since the fall of man, mankind has tried to solve the problems of the world by his own ingenuity. Luther accurately observed that human beings vacillate between pride (the belief that man can solve his own problems) and despair (the view that there is no meaning in the world).

In our time the pendulum has swung to despair. Contemporary man has severed himself from God's revelation and has also abandoned the search for answers to ultimate questions. For this reason, many works of art, though technically excellent, are nevertheless, pagan.

Ever since the time of Sören Kierkegaard, philosophers have accepted irrationalism as a way of life. They believe that we are forced to make decisions in a universe which is basically absurd. Martin Heidegger, a contemporary German philosopher, taught that the individual is thrown rudderless into a world he cannot comprehend rationally; there are no objective grounds to help us make life's choices. As a result, man has *angst* (a vague feeling of dread); yet he must cope with this anxiety by taking a self-authenticating leap in any number of irrational directions.

The effect of this irrationality on art is obvious. If the world is absurd, if there are no answers for modern man, if the best we can do is to live in perpetual despair, art will express this futility.

In exasperation, some non-Christian artists have thought that meaning can be found in sexual freedom. Their works have resulted in blatant pornography. Presumably, the traditions of past centuries hinder man from finding ultimate self-authentication. Of course, all such works of art are outside the realm of Christian aesthetics. The biblical message spells hope, not despair; purity, not sensuality.

Therefore, when we as Christians evaluate a work of art, we must approach it from several perspectives. First, we can judge it according to technical excellence. A work of art could be admired because of the sheer ability it demonstrates, even though its philosophical perspective may be wrong. Second, we can judge the message it is intended to convey. Perhaps the artist wants to highlight the beauty of nature or to picture an event of history. Such legitimate representations may be the product of either a Christian or non-Christian artist. Here, of course, the Christian asks whether the work of art violates the truth of the Word of God. Third, we can decide whether the artist has suited the vehicle to his message. The kind of representation used should be in harmony with the message the artist intended to convey.[3]

Art is indeed a legitimate aspect of our lives, but we must remember that it is only one aspect. It must be seen as a part of the total spectrum of human understanding. The place we give it will vary individually because of our subjective impressions. We should not expect everyone to have the same response to works of art, because we have varying interests and inclinations. Even the brilliant philosopher Plato could not define the word *beauty,* because beauty is "altogether in the eye of the

---

3. For a more detailed discussion of these and other criteria, see Francis A. Schaeffer, *Art and the Bible* (Downers Grove, Ill.: InterVarsity, 1973).

beholder." The problem of definition should remind us that there is latitude for disagreement and personal taste.

One point needs emphasis. Earlier we spoke of the ability of art to communicate, particularily its ability to communicate a world view. In saying this, we must be cautious, because in this regard, art has often been overrated. Art is certainly not the best form of communication. Art can give strength only to what is already known. Without the prior knowledge of the Scriptures, no one would deduce the Gospel of God's grace by viewing the work of Michelangelo in the Sistine Chapel. Gordon Clark, professor of philosophy at Butler University, points out that the cliche "One picture is worth a thousand words" is basically false, although it is true in a blueprint. He appropriately asks, "How many pictures would be required to express the Lord's Prayer or the doctrine of justification by faith?"[4] Art satisfies our taste for an indefinite aesthetic experience and can help express a world view, beyond that, its communicative value is limited in comparison with verbal expression.

Yet, given these limitations, art can be used to accentuate a message. Fresh expressions of art from a Christian perspective are sorely needed. We should not look back to Michelangelo and Raphael and be satisfied. The Christian is the only one who can view the world in focus; he (or she) can be truly creative by being in harmony with the Creator.

---

4. Gordon Clark, "A Christian View of Aesthetics," a paper read at a regional meeting of the Evangelical Theological Society, March 1973.

If art causes tremors, music produces earthquakes. As one frustrated father put it, "One of these days either my son or his stereo is going to be thrown into the street. Right now I don't know which it will be." But if a home is not big enough for both a stereo and a son, some churches are not big enough for a congregation and a youth choir. Emerson's remark, "One man's beauty is another's ugliness," can well be paraphrased, "One man's music is another's noise."

Music itself originated in God's creative work. He created the harmony of musical sounds and the laws of acoustics. Singing and the use of musical instruments are not only sanctioned but commanded in Scripture. At least twelve different musical instruments are referred to in the Old Testament. The psalms particularly are filled with exhortations, "O sing unto the LORD a new song; for he hath done marvellous things; his right hand, and his holy arm, hath gotten him the victory" (Ps 98:1, KJV). Worshiping God with singing is our privilege and duty.

Almost all Christians agree that music should be used in worship. The crunch comes when we try to agree on the kind of music that should be used. Related questions also arise regarding the value of music unaccompanied by words and the effects of popular songs with questionable lyrics.

First, we must recognize that there are different styles in music, which vary according to geographical and cultural eras. For example, the music of John W. Peterson and Ralph Carmichael was considered contemporary in the early sixties. Now their music is considered traditional. Some of the hymns of the Reformation were originally considered too irreverent for the sixteenth century, which was accustomed to the Gregorian chant. Today the popular melodies Luther used are called "the good old hymns."

Parenthetically, we should remember that appreciation for a given type of music is often dependent on our exposure to it. One Christian I know objected to a new song sung by the church choir, and he remarked, "I always like the old songs better." However, in this instance, the song was actually older than the favorite songs of this godly Christian. It usually isn't age but familiarity that determines our taste in hymns.

In every age, the need exists for contemporary songs and the revision of old favorites. Styles in music change; yet often, we are reluctant to accept these changes. One popular hymnal does not contain one hymn by a writer born in this century. Less than one percent of the writers are still living. We should be open to the possibility that God has gifted songwriters today, whose songs are as worthy as those written in past centuries. Age itself does not sanctify.

The first-century church had a variety of musical styles. Paul taught that we should sing "psalms and hymns and spiritual songs." The term *psalms,* is a reference to the Old Testament psalms, which were set to music. Our worship of God would be deepened today if more of the psalms were sung in our worship services. *Hymns* are songs that contain scriptural truth but are of human authorship. This would include the majority of songs in our hymnal today. *Spiritual songs* may include the two previously named categories but possibly refers to songs based on our daily experiences. However, the same expression is also used in the Book of Revelation for songs of worship (Rev 5:9; 14:3; 15:3). Although it may be difficult to identify this third category precisely, Paul encourages believers to use a variety of songs in worship. We should follow his suggestion.

A second observation is that the Scriptures give certain tests as to what content and direction songs should have. For example, songs can be used to (1) worship God (Eph 5:18-19; Col 3:16-17); (2) edify one another (1 Co 14:26); and (3) for the edification of the singer, "Making melody with your heart to the Lord" (Eph 5:18-19). These and other verses teach that the content of the songs should always be scriptural truths. In the Bible, singing is always mentioned in the context of worship and edification.

This leads us to the conclusion that songs must not merely appeal to the emotions but must also convey intellectual content. As Paul put it, "I shall pray with the spirit and I shall pray with the mind also; I shall sing with the spirit and I shall sing with the mind also" (1 Co 14:15). Singing thoughtlessly or singing merely to display technical excellence is wrong. Because singing appeals to emotions, it is possible to give the *impression* that certain ideas are being communicated when nothing intelligent is being said. There is a *feeling* that something is being communicated but that is all—just a feeling.

The notion that songs should be sung for an emotional experience apart from a consideration of the words was exemplified by a remark made by a theologian at Princeton. Francis Schaeffer quotes this professor as remarking that he did not mind saying the creeds as long as he could sing them. What he meant was that as long as he could put the words to music, he did not have to worry about the content.[5] Obviously, he had a sub-biblical view of singing. Words do not become unimportant just because they are set to music.

The exiled Jews in Babylon discovered that they could not sing when in captivity. When their captors demanded songs of them, they responded, "How can we sing the LORD's song in a foreign land?" (Ps 137:4). They realized that singing meant something important. They could not sing simply to produce harmony: the message of the song was too important to be sung glibly. The words were more important than the music.

In fact, music should enhance the words, rather than the words merely providing an excuse to use a certain tune. Since music without words conveys no intellectual content, the words are crucial in singing praise to God and edifying ourselves. Yet, often, songs are selected because of the tune rather than because of the words. But having said this, we must go on to ask what type of music should accompany words.

Here we come face to face with the question of whether scriptural truth can be legitimately sung with certain types of rhythm, such as hard rock or the modern beat. Some Christian singing groups are convinced that the message of the Gospel must be couched in the form of modern man. Ever since Marshall McLuhan proposed the thesis that the medium determines the message, some have assumed that the medium of rock or even hard rock should be used to convey a Christian message. Those who argue for Christian rock point out that styles in music are constantly changing. Coupled with this is the obvious fact that each individual has

---

5. Schaeffer, p. 48.

personal preferences. Conclusion: All types of music are equally legitimate as a means of communicating the Gospel.

However, before we accept this dubious inference, we must remember that it assumes the premise that all types of music are on the same level, and hence personal preference alone is the basis for accepting one form rather than another. Is this true?

One of the problems in discussing this issue is that music is often difficult to classify. As a result, it is often impossible to know just where to draw the line. For example, rock music itself should be distinguished from hard rock, even though the boundaries are often unclear. Here we shall consider primarily hard rock, although what is said may be applied to rock music in general.

A few years ago, researchers discovered that there is a direct relationship between hard rock and premarital sex relationships. Even though the young people could not always understand the words, the music affected their emotional drives. This should not be as surprising as it might seem. In *Cheetah,* a magazine for teenagers, a musician is quoted as saying, "If the establishment knew what today's popular music is really saying, not what the words are saying, but what the music itself is saying, then they would not just turn thumbs down on it. They would ban it, smash all the records and arrest anyone who tried to play it."[6] A leader of a rock group admitted that the loud sounds and the bright lights of today are actually indoctrination tools.

There is little doubt that the rhythm of rock music

---

6. Donald L. LaRose, *The New Sound in Religious Music* (New Life Press, 1971), p. 2.

affects people's emotions in a sensual way. Dr. Joseph Crow, a trumpet player for fifteen years, noted that by changing the rhythm of a song (as pop music does), a psychological response can be created. The result is a hypnotic trance. Everything we hear or see is stored in our brain, and, given the proper stimulus, it can be brought out. Speaking about rock, Crow says, "This music is dangerous whether the young person fully understands the words or not. Music can stimulate the emotions and penetrate the minds in ways that seem incredible."[7]

David Wilkerson, with his wide experience with teenagers, has discovered that young people can become hooked on music almost like those who are hooked on drugs. Addiction to rock music is often a step down on the ladder of moral indifference.

Some young people have told me that they depended on rock music to stifle the conviction of the Holy Spirit. "We'd get out of church in a hurry, get into the car and turn on the rock station full blast. Twenty minutes later we had no desire to get right with God. We felt secure in our old ways."

Bill Gothard explains the effect of music this way: he believes the melody affects our spirit, the harmony (which supports the melody) affects our soul, and the rhythm affects our body. When these are out of balance, music is misused. Music that is directed only to the body produces sensuality, according to his theory.

When rock is linked with a Christian message, the emotional impact of the music overshadows the message. Perhaps the medium is the message but in a different

---

7. Ibid., p. 3.

sense than we think. There are times when the medium dilutes—even negates—the message. Robert Sylvester, commenting on McLuhan's observations of the media, wrote, "All this suggests that the *content* of much of what we say is less important than the act of communication itself. . . . And so media have gone beyond their former role as carrier of messages to become the messages themselves. The medium *is* the message."[8]

This explains why many who have used rock music for evangelism have found that the outward response is overwhelming, but, unfortunately there is not much more than that—an outward response. Sometimes there are tears, but the person doesn't know why he is crying. Like one young person told a counselor, "I had to come forward. Here I am, but I don't know why." The medium has diluted the message.

At any rate, it is apparent that all music is not equal. Styles and forms may vary legitimately, but *certain* rhythms are aimed exclusively toward the emotions and toward the body. When tied to a Christian message, the impact of the Gospel is reduced to an unintelligible emotional response.

Finally, we ask, What about rock music that does not claim any Christian message but is decidedly non-Christian or, more accurately, pagan? Enough has been said to show that it will have a detrimental effect on those who listen to it. Earlier, we noted that the words of these songs are often unintelligible, but it is important to note that when the lyrics are understood, the message is often one filled with double meanings, inuendo, and

---

8. Robert Sylvester, "The Cool World of Marshall McLuhan," *Interaction,* October 1968.

sensuality. The words and music are calculated to break down the moral resistance of those who listen. Twenty-two psychologists and psychiatrists from leading educational institutions compiled a report about the young generation. According to them, rock music says in effect, "Come, swing with me." In other words, "It is aimed specifically at a possible sex partner and is a thinly disguised proposition."[9]

For those addicted to rock music, there is deliverance through Christ; for those who have not as yet accepted it, an ounce of prevention is worth a pound of cure. By being exposed to music designed to enrich rather than degrade, one may escape the emotional and spiritual impact of music calculated to rid him of sexual inhibitions.

What part should music have in our lives? It was created by God to aid us in our worship and edification. It can appeal to our sense of harmony and artistic beauty. But like everything else that man touches, it can become twisted and corrupted. Although we can appreciate the music of Bach (since it appeals to the whole man), the scriptural purpose of music is to enrich our worship of God and to increase spiritual edification. All music must be judged according to this high biblical standard.

---

9. LaRose, p. 3.

PART III

Finding God's Direction in the World's Conflicts

11

THE TENSIONS OF DOCTRINE

WHEN WE LOVE the world of men but shun the world system, we are immediately involved in a curious conflict. We encounter a variety of pressures, all competing for our allegiance. For example, when we love people we will be tempted to compromise our doctrine to accommodate those who have deviant or even heretical views.

As a reaction to such pressure, some orthodox churches believe that doctrinal purity necessitates a form of isolationism from the moral and spiritual milieu of our day. In extreme cases, some churches believe that they have sole possession of the truth and only those who agree with them are the spiritual remnant of this age. Like Elijah, they are convinced that they alone have refused to bow the knee to Baal. But perhaps they, like the prophet also, have greatly underestimated the number of true prophets God has preserved.

On the other hand, some churches and individuals have become involved in directly penetrating the world and, in their enthusiasm, have neglected necessary doctrinal matters. As a result, their effectiveness has been weakened because their theology has been watered down.

Both extremes are to be avoided. Our love for the world should not make us disregard doctrinal content;

nor should we believe that only those who agree with us in every detail deserve our fellowship and support.

DOCTRINAL SEPARATION

The Scriptures teach that doctrinal integrity must play a vital part in wholesome penetration of the world. This balance will rescue us from a sentimentalism that is willing to disregard doctrinal differences in the interest of serving love. On the other hand, we must be reminded that doctrinal purity is not an excuse to be isolated from social, moral, and spiritual needs of our time. Nor does it necessitate a rigid conformity to every detail of a given doctrinal position.

In order to maintain balance, we must remember that our love for one another and the world should not make us ignore doctrinal matters. We have all heard the plea, "If we could just set aside our doctrinal differences and show love and unity, we'd win the world to Christ." There is little doubt that petty doctrinal issues have often been blown out of proportion, and theological disagreements frequently give the world a distasteful picture of Christianity. Our disagreements cannot be ignored, but the way we handle them should be an example of love and Christian concern.

At what places must lines be clearly drawn? Love cannot tolerate organic unity with those whose fundamental views are distorted. Under the guise of love, evangelical churches have cooperated in evangelistic endeavors with liberal churches. Seminaries which were founded on the basis of orthodoxy have shifted to a position that denies the authority of Scripture. Those who have opposed such changes are often labeled "heresy hunters" or "belligerent." Presumably, love should cover a variety of doctrinal opinions. The argument that love should make us tolerant of all sorts of doctrinal perspectives is powerful, since it implies that orthodox churches are engaged in irrelevant hair-splitting while the needs of people are ignored.

How do we answer the charge that insisting on doctrinal and moral purity is contrary to the love that we should have for all men? The answer is to understand the meaning of the word *love*. Love is not to be equated with sentimentality; nor is it synonymous with tolerance. We often get the impression that the lenient are loving and the strict are unloving, but this is not the teaching of the New Testament. Love cannot bend to doctrine, and right doctrine can never be achieved without love. This is why the phrase "dead orthodoxy" is essentially a contradiction. We cannot be dead and truly orthodox at the same time.

Significantly, the book of 2 John, which contains a stern warning to false teachers and instructs believers that heretics should neither be received nor greeted, anticipates the twentieth-century notion that intolerance is contrary to love. John defines love in a single sentence: "And this is love, that we walk according to His commandments" (2 Jn 6). In other words, love is defined as obedience to God's commands. If we censure false teachers and refrain from bidding them godspeed, we are (contrary to popular opinion) exercising love. Of course, such action should not be taken with an attitude of vindictiveness or superiority. It is possible to be correct doctrinally and have the wrong attitude toward those who are in error. Some Christians seem to take delight in using a magnifying glass to find fault; others, equally orthodox, handle error with a concerned attitude of love. The scriptural balance is "speaking the truth in love" (Eph 4:15). This means that we must not merely be correct theologically but be correct emotionally as well. But if we guard the doctrine of Christ from misrepresentation, and if we defend the faith delivered to the saints, we have done the will of God. And *that* is love.

An example of how love cannot be allowed to produce tolerance for sin or doctrinal impurity is found in the nature of God. Since God is love, He did not want the entire human race to be lost in hell. Yet, this did not mean that He could wipe our slate clean so that His loving desire would be satisfied. He could not compromise His justice or His hatred of sin. Therefore, He provided a method of redemption whereby He could maintain His justice and yet fulfill His loving wish for mankind. Christ became the propitiation (satisfaction) for sin, so that God could be just and, at the same time, declare sinners righteous (Ro 3:26). In this way, His attributes were not compromised. Love can never lead to tolerance for sin or heretical doctrine; nor can doctrine replace love.

Where should we draw the line? We must begin with the doctrine of Christ. Paul the apostle insisted that the trumpet of the gospel be sounded with clarity. Writing to the Galatians, who were tempted to follow those who distort the doctrine of Christ (i.e., those who wanted to add works to the Gospel of grace), Paul warned, "But even though we, or an angel from heaven, should preach to you a gospel contrary to that which we have preached to you, let him be accursed" (Gal 1:8). Then, lest the Galatians should think that they did not hear him correctly, the apostle repeats the same words in the next sentence. Paul wanted his readers to understand that there are not two versions of the Gospel; the Gospel the Galatians began to follow was really not another: there was only one version of the message. This verse alone should be sufficient to guard us from thinking that everyone who "proclaims Christ" is to be accepted without further reservations. We must make certain that the content of the message is accurate. Is Christ preached as the One whose merit alone is sufficient for salvation, or is He merely our example to which we must add our good works for salvation? Without specific content, the name *Christ* can be used (or rather, misused) to encompass any ideology, heresy, or pet project that anyone might happen to choose. In our day, the banner of love is used to tolerate a broad spectrum of "other gospels." Paul reminds us that if someone does not proclaim the Gospel of Christ as revealed in the Scriptures, such an individual is to be shunned.

The apostle John taught the same truth in equally vivid terms. He wrote that those who do not acknowledge Jesus Christ as coming in the flesh are deceivers and antichrist. Teachers who come to a church and do not bring the scriptural teaching of Christ should not be received into a home nor given a greeting, for such an encouragement makes the believer a participant in the false teacher's evil deeds (2 Jn 7-11). Added to these passages are extended sections in 2 Peter 2 and the Epistle of Jude, which are directed at false teachers. Although such apostates are sure to come into the church, believers should reject them and their heretical teachings. In a passage somewhat difficult to interpret, Jude teaches that we should have mercy on those who pervert the teaching of Christ and that our aim should be to fearfully snatch them out of the fire, making certain that we ourselves are undefiled (vv. 22-23). These and other passages teach that we cannot have unity with those who do not hold to the scriptural teaching of Christ. From such, we should separate ourselves.

It is popular to think that churches would have a greater impact on the world if they were united organically. Not necessarily. Churches that have drifted from the deity of Christ and substitutionary atonement can have a greater social impact on the world if united; but union will not give them spiritual life. Someone has accurately observed that putting a group of graveyards together will not produce a resurrection. And Evangelicals who turn to such churches for help in evangelism or strength have turned from the living God to a dead corpse.

FELLOWSHIP IN CHRIST

What about those who hold to a scriptural doctrine of Christ but do not believe in the inerrancy of Scripture? Or those whose eschatology (prophecy) is different from ours? Paul taught that all scriptural teachings were necessary (1 Ti 4:11-16; 6:3-5; 2 Ti 3:14-17). We should not conclude that other doctrines, such as eternal punishment (Mt 25:46) or the trustworthiness of the Old Testament, are negotiable (Mt 5:18). Even so, we can have fellowship with all those who are members of Christ's Body through faith in Him.

Yet we must realize that we can have fellowship with others only to the extent that we are able to share a common life with them (which is the meaning of the

156

word *fellowship*). For example, we can have a certain type of fellowship with all men, since we share the common experience of life. But with those who do not understand the things of God, our fellowship is limited. The next level of fellowship is that which we can have with all Christians. Regardless of doctrinal or denominational differences, all who have trusted Christ are a part of His body, and therefore, we can have meaningful fellowship with them. Also, our responsibility to Christians is greater than it is to the non-Christian world. Paul writes, "So then, while we have opportunity, let us do good to all men, and especially to those who are of the household of the faith" (Gal 6:10). Then, within the larger sphere of Christians, there are smaller circles of fellowship. It is in these particular groups that we are able to have the deepest level of mutual sharing, not merely because we have greater fellowship with those that we know best, but also because we can have better fellowship with those who share our doctrinal views.

Those who believe in baptism by immersion would not feel comfortable in a service where infant baptism took place. Yet both groups, who emphasize salvation through Christ alone and other basic doctrines, can have truly beautiful fellowship despite their differences regarding the mode of baptism. We should not expect all Christians to agree regarding the interpretation of Scripture, nor should we expect blind conformity. We must be willing to allow for individual differences and at the same time recognize that other circles of fellowship exist.

Logically, we should choose a church whose doctrines correspond most closely to what we believe is the teaching of the Scriptures. And while we should love all others, we need not agree with them. In fact, we would not be true to our calling if we did.

Let's be specific. Suppose that an evangelical seminary deviates from its original doctrinal position and teaches that the Scriptures are not inerrant but contain some historical and scientific blunders. At the same time, those who teach such error might be men who display the fruit of the Spirit and are genuinely concerned about others. There is no question about their commitment to Christ. What should our response be? The most popular course of action is to let love (or what is thought to be love) rule. Those who may object to the school's position are usually accused of being divisive or obstinate or both. Misunderstandings develop, and each side is more convinced than ever that they will not budge. So the easy way out is to stop rocking the boat. In the interest of unity, we might let the matter rest.

Except for one fact. Many existing liberal schools began with a distinct Christian commitment. They began the toboggan slide when they began to question whether the Bible is completely trustworthy. They realized that if the Bible erred historically, there was no reason to believe it was reliable on spiritual matters either. A few generations later, it was just another book. Thus while individuals can sincerely love Christ and yet deny inerrancy, a religious body cannot tolerate such a position indefinitely. The next generation will argue for more consistency, until an error is pushed to its logical conclusion.

Therefore, love will not tolerate such doctrinal deviation. *But love will attempt to resolve the disagreement in the right spirit and with transparent honesty.* Love will not distort the truth; nor will it seek self-glory; nor will it seek vindication. During times of disagreement, love will receive its ultimate test. If we love our brothers when differences exist, this is surely a testimony to the supernatural power of Christ.

So the fact of disagreements regarding premillennialism, eternal security, and inspiration should be faced realistically and honestly. Such matters should not be ignored. But these differences provide an opportunity to display the love of Christ, not merely to those who agree with us but to those who disagree as well. We may be convinced that a group of believers is in error; they might believe the same about us. As differences are discussed and defended, attitudes of humility and genuine concern should prevail.

Sometimes we are faced with the question of how we should respond to believers who are in liberal churches. Some have trusted Christ but have continued their ministry in denominational groups which have officially abandoned orthodoxy. Paul taught that we ought to separate ourselves from every brother who leads an unruly life and not according to the traditions which the apostle proclaimed (2 Th 3:6). Yet it is possible that some are following the scriptural doctrines within the confines of a liberal denomination, even though we might feel they are disobeying the command to "come out from among them and be separate." Perhaps we cannot specify what our attitude should be in every case. Sometimes there are those who are proclaiming Christ clearly without compromise despite a given denominational label. Others (especially weak Christians) may not realize that their group has compromised the Scriptures. So we must treat each case with wisdom, attempting to help others see the need for doctrinal purity and separation from those who have denied the faith.

A final word. We must make a distinction between personal fellowship and organic unity. The leader of a prominent evangelical organization told how he met a fellow believer in what can be confidently described as an apostate denomination. They put their arms around each other as brothers in Christ. Undoubtedly, this was a genuine expression of their mutual faith. But in publicizing that act, the impression was given (perhaps unwittingly) that we ought to open our eyes to the similarities we have with liberal groups rather than concentrate on our differences. Since God has His children everywhere, we should be willing to accept other groups (liberal or not) despite our doctrinal differences.

It is true God has His children everywhere—even in unlikely places. And since they are a part of Christ's Body, we should love them. But to conclude or even to give the impression that we can, on this basis, broaden fellowship or cooperation with liberal groups is false. Wherever we find a believer, we ought to rejoice. But because a liberal group happens to have a few believers, that fact should not make us more lenient towards teachings that deviate from the basic facts of the Gospel. Christ prayed that all who believe on Him would be one. But this unity is not the kind that can be brought about by discarding differences or compromising doctrine. In Christ, we have a unity that transcends the mere external act of outward organization or intellectual agreement. Christ's prayer has been answered because we are all members of His Body. On a practical level, this unity can be displayed to the world by the way in which we handle our minor differences; we don't all have to believe the same on all points to achieve it. We can have marginal doctrinal differences and still cause the world to exclaim, "Behold how they love one another!" And that, only a living God can enable us to achieve!

12

GOD'S COMPASS POINTS UP

ONE OF MY CLASSMATES in college believed that he was in love with two girls at the same time (perhaps a more welcome predicament for him than for the girls). How could he know which one (if either) he should marry? In church, he heard, "The will of God is found in the Bible." Initially, that sounded comforting, until he discovered that neither of the girl's names is mentioned on its pages.

A student sent his application to three colleges. He told the Lord that he would go to the one that accepted him. It sounded like a wise move, but, unfortunately, he was accepted by all three. "So now what do I do?" he blurted. A good question.

Living in this world demands that we make choices; not merely choices between good and evil but choices between two seemingly equal goods. If we are not careful, we might hastily conclude that the Bible is not much help in making decisions where good and evil are not the real issues. Or else we can make the opposite mistake of trying to torture the Bible into giving us specific geographical guidance.

We've all heard stories about Christians who have been miraculously led by opening their Bible at random. I heard of one man who flopped his Bible open, and the first word he saw was *north,* so he set out to be a missionary in Alaska. I tried that once when I was in high school; I pointed my unguided finger at the strangest verses, but God's leading was as confusing as ever. It simply did not work. But time does not wait for us. We must make choices.

Many of us look back with envy at the days of the Old Testament when God often spoke directly to men. Abram was called out of Ur of the Chaldees by a direct command of God. Gideon put out his fleece, and God used it to make His will clear. Now if we had directions like that, we would know what to do; but in today's world, all the signals are confused, muddy, and blurred. There isn't much joy in going from pillar to post, hoping that God will make the best of whatever we are doing. Is there a way out of the fog? Is it possible for a Christian to know God's will and enjoy doing it? Yes. And God wants that possibility to be a reality.

THREE MISCONCEPTIONS

Unfortunately, some Christians think of the will of God almost solely in geographical terms (does God want me in Chicago or Atlanta?) But geographical questions are secondary, or—more accurately—they are minor, compared to the weightier matters of God's will. Choosing a country or locality is necessary and often frustrating, but such decisions will follow quite naturally once more basic questions have been clearly answered.

A second misconception of a host of Christians is that the will of God refers only to special vocations. So, God directs only missionaries, pastors, and other Christian workers (usually in that order), but His direction has no relationship to plumbers, factory workers, taxi drivers, and garbage collectors. Perhaps we are still living with the notion that washing dishes, digging ditches, and weeding a garden can never merit eternal reward. Only teaching a Sunday school class, witnessing, or preaching a sermon will receive honorable mention at the judgment seat. But in God's sight, our occupation is not nearly as significant as our motivation and obedience. Every Christian's employer is God, so whatever we do in the familiar routine of life should be done in His name (Col 3:17). Our attitude and faithfulness determine our reward.

It is true that those in vocational Christian work may have a distinct calling of God. To be a prophet in the Old Testament or a preacher in this age does demand special gifts and involves more responsibility than may be required for other vocations. For example, James warns, "Let not many of you become teachers, my brethren, knowing that as such we shall incur a stricter judgment" (3:1). But even with these distinctions, each Christian, regardless of how humanly insignificant his occupation or how famous his achievements, has an equal opportunity to please God by the faithful use of his gifts. On this basis, all members of the Body of Christ stand on equal ground.

My point is that every Christian can have the satisfaction of doing God's will. There will be no second-class citizens at the judgment seat of Christ. The basis of judgment will be obedience to *what* God wanted us to do and *how* we did it. This evaluation will have little or no resemblance to our human standards of success.

A third misconception is that some consider the will of God to be so mysterious (now you see it, now you don't) that they are led to despair. The will of God, which is designed to be good, acceptable, and perfect, turns out to be frustrating and elusive. A deeply spiritual (though misinformed) missionary I know used to pray for special guidance about the most trivial matters. She would even try to decide whether it was God's will that she wash her hair on a given evening. She was right in understanding that God is interested in the mundane affairs of life, but she was wrong in believing that she always needed a special sign. Obviously she was a mental wreck. She did not realize that the will of God is simply living in obedience to whatever lies ahead. His guidance is not mysterious. In short, if your hair needs washing, wash it!

AN ILLUSTRATION

God told Jonah to go to Ninevah. Unlike many of us, the prophet had the benefit of explicit instructions. He knew what he should do (preach) and he knew where to do it (Ninevah). But communication is not the most difficult problem God encounters when He directs us. A greater problem is our disobedience.

Evidently, Jonah decided to escape to Tarshish, because he felt that Assyria would destroy Israel if Nineveh (the capital city) repented. So Jonah heroically risked his life in disobedience, hoping to spare God's chosen people. The decision seemed noble, but it was also sinful.

When he arrived at Joppa, he found a ship ready to leave for Tarshish. This coincidence probably confirmed his decision to disobey God's command. Perhaps he thought, *God has provided this ship, given me money*

165

*to pay for the ticket, and there is room for one more.
These circumstances are of God.* The first lesson we
learn from Jonah is that a coincidence alone does not
guarantee that we have made a correct choice.

I heard a student say, "But I just happened to meet
her. It was miraculous. My plane flight was canceled,
and so I stayed in Seattle a few days and we met. I'm
sure our marriage is God's will." But Jonah reminds
us that no set of circumstances or unusual events is
confirmation of God's will if we are violating a clear
command. A Christian who marries a non-Christian is
out of God's will no matter how miraculously they met.
A canceled plane flight does not necessarily confirm
God's will. Nor does a feeling that "we get along so well
together." *Nothing* can justify disobedience. Not even
loving concern.

What happened to Jonah next? Did God abandon him?
Since God's command to him had been so clear, it
would have been reasonable for God to have said, "Jonah, I'm finished with you. I'll get someone else." But
He did not.

In fact, He went to a great deal of trouble. Specifically, God (1) created a storm; (2) loaded the dice of
the sailors so that Jonah (rather than another man) was
thrown into the sea; (3) appointed a great fish to swal-
low Jonah; (4) controlled the digestion of the fish so
that it vomited Jonah onto the dry land. That's doing
a lot for someone who was flagrantly disobedient .This
leads us to a second observation: God is more concerned about keeping us in His will than we are to be
kept in it! We often mistakenly get the impression that
God expects us to walk such a fine line that we are never
sure we are in His will. And if we make one mistake,

166

we think that we might never get back onto the track. We believe that the will of God is a deep mystery that God delights to hide from us. Only those with a high degree of spirituality have a chance of finding His elusive plan.

If God went through such pains to bring a prophet (who knew His will clearly) back into His plan, think of what He will do for a Christian who wants to do the will of God but is temporarily confused as to what it is! God is well qualified to guide a willing heart.

Ponder this for a moment: was Jonah in the will of God in the belly of the fish? The answer is no, for he had been scheduled to go to Nineveh. But because he disobeyed, God did provide a special storm and a tailor-made fish to intercept His servant. In this secondary sense, Jonah was now in God's will: God manipulated circumstances and events so that Jonah ended up where God wanted him—in the belly of a fish.

God can take any situation—even our mistakes and failures—and make the best of it. Even our sins can be incorporated into His plan, so that all things work together for good. Of course this does not justify sin. There are serious consequences for disobedience. But God can use such experiences to teach us some needed lessons.

A girl came to me with a problem. "I've married the wrong man. I knew I should not have done it. The only way out is divorce." Whether she married the "wrong one" or not, I cannot say. But her attitude alone was sufficient to break up their marriage. Even if she had married the wrong man (a flimsy supposition), she failed to see that God is able to use that relationship to work out His purposes. Of course, that might involve

167

radical adjustments, suffering, and spiritual strain (since all disobedience has its price, as Jonah learned). But God can pick up the pieces and incorporate them into His plan.

The same can be said for those who are out of God's will geographically. One Christian *knew* God wanted him in Europe but ended up as a salesman in Canada. In later years, he wanted to go to Europe, but it was too late. He began a business at a service station and witnessed to everyone who came by. Two of his children became missionaries. He has lived a successful Christian life. Assuming that God did originally call him to Europe, is he in God's will now? Once again, we must say no, but because of God's goodness, we can say yes too!

God does not want us to live in the past! I have known Christians who have lived with deep regret because of a wrong choice made years before. They have come to Christ for forgiveness, but they are still plagued with guilt. They can trust Christ to forgive some sins but not all; the past is always with them. They have forgotten that the purpose of the cross is to repair the irreparable. A third lesson from Jonah: it is never too late to begin again; regardless of the past, we can be in the will of God *today*.

All of us make mistakes through ignorance or disobedience or both. But God never runs out of plans. He never says, "You blew it. You are not where I intended; I can't work you in anywhere else." God is never caught off guard. He has multiple contingency plans which He has already ordained to use. He will create fish, cause storms, and even use loaded dice to keep His children on the course.

Perhaps you felt uneasy about the story of Jonah. After all, he knew explicitly what God wanted him to do. How simple it would be if God were to speak to us directly, then we could be sure that we were making wise decisions! I have good news for you: He *does!*

God's will is given to us verbally and directly. It is spelled out for us numerous times in the New Testament. For example, He wants us to put our trust in Christ (Jn 6:28-29); to give ourselves as a living sacrifice (Ro 12:1-2); not to try to please men but to please God (Eph 6:5-6); and to give thanks in everything (1 Th 5:18). *This* is the will of God.

"But" someone says, "we've already agreed that the Bible does not specify whom we are to marry, what our vocation should be, and where we should live." True. But *obedience to revealed truth guarantees guidance in matters unrevealed.* If we submit to the will of God as we read it in His Word, God is obligated (because of His promises) to guide us vocationally and geographically. There is a direct connection between our obedience to the commands of Scripture and God's guidance in the often unclear choices of everyday life.

David tells us about this relationship in Psalm 32. He describes his distress before he confessed his sin (vv. 3-4). After confession, he breaks out in praise to God and is assured of the promise, "I will instruct you and teach you in the way which you should go; I will counsel you with My eye upon you" (v. 8). The assurance of God's guidance came when David cleansed his life from sin. The next verse cautions, "Do not be as the horse or as the mule which have no understanding; Whose trappings include bit and bridle to hold them in check." We thwart God's guidance by unconfessed sin; it is restored by confession.

Romans 12:1-2 makes a similar point. Giving our bodies as a living sacrifice and refusing to be conformed to this world is the prerequisite to proving what is the good, acceptable, and perfect will of God. As in the life of Jonah, the greatest obstacle to guidance is disobedience or resistance to what God requires. I have known Bible school students who skipped missionary prayer meetings for fear that they might be "called" to Africa. Some Christian fellows and girls are unwilling to give God their future because they are convinced God will not give them a partner.

Often we are tempted to make choices on the basis of a worldly scale of values. We choose homes, cars, and vocations solely for prestige. When this happens, we lose a conscious sense of doing everything as unto God and not unto man. Like David, we have no assurance of God's guidance.

God's will for us is just as specific as the command given to Jonah, although its *content* is different. God's compass does not spin in a variety of confusing directions. He does not delight in our frustration when three possibilities open up before us, except, of course, when such frustration drives us to Him. His compass points upward, to Himself; our vertical relationship with Him is more important than the horizontal (earthly) decisions we face every day. That is why Christ promised that if we seek first God's Kingdom and His righteousness, the needs of life would be supplied.

How does God direct us? Not with a blinding light from heaven nor a verse of Scripture selected at random. We commit our way unto Him and do whatever lies at hand, and He will control circumstances, change our inclinations, and lead us into opportunities which will be part of the divine plan. Also, he leads us to people who have the wisdom to give us counsel.

Do you feel inclined to be a missionary? Pursue the matter, and if you are wrong, God is obligated to stop you from making a wrong choice. Do you have three colleges you could attend? Be willing to go to any one of them. Then select the one that seems to best fit in with your pocketbook, interests, and location. If you have committed your way to God, He will stop you from making a wrong choice. Maybe He will make you uneasy about one school or close the door to another. He has an unlimited number of ways to lead us. Relax. Commit your way to Him. God has no difficulty in guiding a willing and obedient servant.

God's will is good, acceptable, and perfect. We need not fear it. Once we have decided that we are willing to do whatever He wants and to live in light of biblical commands, we step out in faith. He will intercept us when we make a mistake. Of course, if we are disobedient to the Scriptures, we will be disciplined. It might take a storm, a fish, and a desperate prayer, but He will be willing to redirect our steps.

God has a great investment in every Christian. He is interested in every detail of our lives. He wants us to make the small decisions as well as the big ones in dependence upon Him. This takes more faith than if He were to direct us visibly. Anyone can follow a blinding light; it takes greater faith to trust solely in God's promise. Make your decisions today by remembering that God places more emphasis on the spiritual than the geographical. Once we have settled our basic attitude toward Him (willing obedience), He has promised to take it from there. To put it concisely, "Trust in the LORD with all your heart, And do not lean on your own understanding. In all your ways acknowledge Him, and He will make your paths straight" (Pr 3:5-6).

He did a lot for a disobedient prophet. He won't do less for an obedient servant. Remember, the compass points up.

13

THE AX PUT TO THE ROOT OF THE TREE

I MET A GIRL named Karen at a youth retreat. "I need some help because my life is a bit messed up," she modestly admitted. She was experiencing continual failure in her Christian life. Specifically, she told me that she had five problems: sexual looseness, drinking, smoking, swearing, and bitterness against her parents. She stared defiantly into space wondering what to say next. I must admit I was not fully prepared for her next remark. In tears she added, "I'll have you know that I've come to Christ ten times with these problems, and He hasn't helped me a bit." Ten times she had come to the One who claimed to deliver people from their sins. But for Karen it had not worked.

There are hundreds of Karens trying to live the Christian life. As they become older, they eventually outgrow some of the sins of their youth, but their life remains as empty as before. The pleasures of youth give way to the desire for status; bitterness toward their parents leads to bitterness against their marriage partner; the habits which were practiced just for kicks in their youth have now ensnared them. Their sins may not be as obvious, but their defeat is just as real. Like Karen, they too have stood in a dedication service to sing, "I surrender all," but it has not helped much, at least not for long.

Everyone feels at times like Karen did. I have. On the one hand, I have read of God's power; on the other hand, I have seen the failures in my life and wondered where the breakdown between the two occurs. One of the most practical questions that we all face is how to translate God's promises into spiritual victory and personal fulfillment.

A minister's wife admitted candidly, "Ministers often leave a church essentially as they found it. They come and go, but the lives of the people remain the same. Those who sought status, money, or personal pleasure haven't changed even after years of sermons." Unfortunately, this woman spoke the truth. Spiritual growth cannot be measured with a yardstick, but we cannot escape the suspicion that many who are exposed to biblical truth are not being changed by it. Why?

One reason is that we often adjust the outer fringes of our life to conform to the truth we hear. For example, when we are reminded that we should read and study the Scriptures, we may become convicted and begin to meditate on the Word. But two weeks later, our determination has waned, and we lapse back into our former ways. Once again, we can go for days without reading the Bible or saying more than a routine prayer. Later, we may be challenged to witness, and we begin to share our faith. But it lasts only for a time. We can follow this pattern for years and make little progress, simply because the core of our motivation and basic goals has remained the same despite minor adjustments.

It's also easy to become immune to truth. We don't believe the ads on television, and we view the biblical promises with the same suspicion. We begin to believe (perhaps rightly so) that there is very little that can be said that we haven't heard before. Like Karen, we've tried it but it hasn't worked.

At other times, we may not even be aware that we are out of step with Christ. The philosopher Descartes reminded us that it is possible to be asleep while dreaming we are awake, perhaps like the minister who dreamed he was preaching and then woke up and found out he was! The people of Laodicea thought they were in need of nothing but did *not know* that they were wretched, miserable, poor, blind, and naked (Rev 3:17). We can be asleep spiritually and yet be convinced we are wide awake. In such instances, only a tragedy or sudden emergency can bring us to our senses. Then we are forced to evaluate our priorities.

These are the symptoms, but is there a cure? Is there hope for Karen? For you? For me?

THE STRUGGLE OF THE WILL

When Christ was on earth, did He do what He *wanted* to do? Yes. And no. Christ had a passion to do the will of the Father. The prospect of being nailed to a cross outside the walls of Jerusalem was not glamorous. The Father's blueprint called for a shameful death, but Christ did not quibble over the plan. He was obedient in death and could say with the psalmist, "I delight to do thy will, O God." Christ's only concern was the Father's will.

Yet we must see Christ's commitment from another perspective. Paul wrote, "For even Christ pleased not himself" (Ro 15:3, KJV). This doesn't mean that

Christ was displeased with the Father's will, but rather that He was willing to set aside all personal considerations to finish the assignment He had been given. To put it another way, Christ didn't ask, What pleases me? but, What pleases the Father? And if the Father was pleased, the Son was pleased. The will of God is *all* that mattered. And He is our model of commitment.

Whenever we are faced with a crucial decision, our generation has been taught to ask, What's in it for me? Will it give me pleasure? Profit? Security? Fulfillment? We are not necessarily opposed to God; we just fit Him in wherever He is able to help *us*. The idea that our wills should be subjected to His control, even when our personal ambitions are at stake, is not easy to accept. We can assent mentally to God's control, but in practice, we might still spend our lives pleasing ourselves.

How do we begin to let God be in control? We must give Him our bodies—our mind, talents, sex drive, and reputation. We (our total self) must be given to Him in a conscious act of commitment. This is difficult, so difficult that we will use any excuse to avoid the implications of such an act.

This is why Karen was not able to live a joyful Christian life, even though she had "come to Christ ten times." I asked if she would be willing to give herself to God so that He could actually change her desires, dissolve the bitterness, and simply take charge. She considered the implications of this and then answered thoughtfully, "I don't want to forgive my parents. I have a right to be bitter." I explained that commitment meant more than forgiving her parents. God should have control over her future. She would have to recognize that He might lead her to become a missionary, or perhaps she would remain unmarried. But in return for letting God be in charge, she would be rewarded with a sense of fulfillment, victory, and peace. Her response was enlightening. "I expected you to simply pray for me," she explained. "If I have to give myself to God completely, if it means submitting myself to Him in the sense you mean, I'm not prepared for that." Karen left with her five problems. She had indeed come to Christ nearly a dozen times: she had come because she thought He would help her stay out of trouble while she was pleasing herself. But when it came down to the moment of truth, she backed off. Giving ourselves to God is not easy.

Let's take our reputation as another example of continual struggle. On a plane, I met a man who was the director of a Christian organization. He told me about the pressure he faces in traveling from city to city. By virtue of his position, people had high expectations of him, and he had to make certain never to disappoint them. So he had to maintain his reputation. He was bound by the approval of men. The joy of his salvation was gone. He was not a free man.

Consider the minister who is relieved to discover that church attendance was down during his vacation; he rejoices that the people respond to his ministry with more enthusiasm than they do for someone else. He is not able to thank God for those who have gifts that are greater than his.

Then there are parents who are constantly protecting their reputation. If a child sins, they do not discipline him because he did evil in the sight of God but because he ruined the family name. They become so conscious of their image that their wayward son is not welcome in church if he should walk in with shaggy hair and wearing jeans. "Think of what you have done to *us,*" they complain.

Our reputations *are* important, and each of us needs a proper self-image. But paradoxically, when we try to polish our reputation, we lose it; when we give it to Christ, we gain it. When we finally let the facade fall, we find freedom in our relationship with God and with one another. Image-building, the hallmark of worldliness, will finally be over.

Commitment to Christ means a radical change in perspective. Our priorities will be changed when we finally submit our will to God. And even then the struggle will not be over. Each day the initial commitment must be reaffirmed as new matters will be transferred to God's control.

Christ is our example of obedience. We will never approach the measure of His commitment to do the Father's will. But our first feeble step toward freedom from the sins that plague us occurs when we say, 'Not my will but Yours." I've found it tough to say that and mean it. But it must be said—and meant.

THE STRUGGLE FOR POWER

Let's suppose we have made the basic decision to submit ourselves to God. What happens next? We are to live by faith in dependence on the Holy Spirit. Christ is our example of how to operate while depending on the strength of Another. Christ did nothing on His own. He let the Father work *through* Him. On numerous occasions, He reminded His listeners that the Father was doing the work (Jn 5:17, 19; 14:10). Even the words

178

which He spoke were not His but had been given to Him by the Father (Jn 12:49). This quality of dependence illustrates the Christian life.

Many who read the gospels are puzzled to find that Christ frequently went up to a mountain to pray and sometimes prayed all night. Since He was God, why did He need to be strengthened spiritually? Why did He repeatedly say He did nothing of Himself?

Although Christ is God, He lived as man. Let us imagine that a millionaire were to decide to identify with the people in the poorest section of the city. He would walk to work with them, eat with them, and work at the same job. He would live on the wages he earned for the week. At any time, he could write out a large check, live in a beautiful home, and lie in the sun every afternoon. But he doesn't. He does not depend on his wealth in the bank. He lives as the poor do, even though he is a millionaire.

Similarly, Christ, though having all the attributes of Deity, lived as we do.[1] He voluntarily gave up the independent use of His attributes of Deity and lived as God intended man to live—in total dependence on the Father. Christ is the last Adam; He lived as God intended the first Adam to live.

Christ gave His disciples a clear command to follow His example. He said, "As the living Father sent Me, and I live because of the Father, so he who eats Me, he also shall live because of Me" (Jn 6:57). Christ intends

---

1. As all illustrations of the incarnation, this one has its limitations. In some cases there is evidence that Christ did exercise the use of His attributes of Deity, such as when He displayed omniscience. The relationship between His two natures has always been a mystery. But in general, this illustration shows how Christ, though fully God, lived as man.

that the same relationship He had with His Father be ours with Him. As He lived, so we are to live. This means that we are to do everything in faith, abiding in Christ's strength, because without Him, we can do nothing that will count for eternity. Unfortunately, we sometimes think of living by faith in financial matters, but everything we do—whether we eat, drink, or write a book on worldliness—must be done with an attitude of dependence on Christ who alone can please the Father through us.

The reality of Christ's power is brought to us by the power of the Holy Spirit. We will not be able to face the temptations of the world nor cope with the tensions of our age unless we are filled (controlled) by the Holy Spirit. He wants to display power through us, but He is squelched through unbelief and sin.

Today we are bombarded with conflicting (and confusing) views of the Holy Spirit. Many Christians are convinced that the answer to their emptiness is to have a crisis experience which will revolutionize their lifestyle. Until that "happening," they have accepted their defeat as inevitable. Those who have the experience (which may have a variety of labels attached to it) believe that they have found the key to supernatural power. In the confusion, one fact is overlooked: any Christian can display the supernatural fruit of the Spirit to the extent that he lives in dependence on the Holy Spirit who indwells him (or her). In other words, there is no hidden secret nor additional spiritual experience that we must have. Undoubtedly, we often learn dependence by means of a crisis experience; but the attitude of dependence and not the experience itself is the key to spiritual victory.

Living by faith (dependence) is more easily talked about than done. I find it easier to explain how to live the Christian life than to do it myself, for one good reason: my sinful nature balks at dependence and prefers independence. This is why growth and development are necessary for us all. We never get to the point where we can say "I've finally arrived."

One point needs emphasis: we cannot look to ourselves (our emotions, determination, or good qualities) for spiritual power. Supernatural power resides in Christ and the work which He has already *finished*. Because of our identification with Him, sins need not have control over us.[2]

Let me illustrate. Because of a misunderstanding, I was angry with a man whom I thought had wronged me. My anger was sin. It affected my attitude not only to this man but to everyone else. Even though I knew I was sinning, I had no control over my emotions. Even praying for victory didn't help. Then I remembered the objective fact of victory in Christ, the fact that *this* sin was already conquered on the cross; I realized that victory was *legally* mine despite the way I felt emotionally. From that moment on, my anger began to subside, and later the bitterness was gone—much to my surprise! I found that the greatest struggle was to trust the power of Christ even when I was coming apart emotionally.

God is powerful and wants to prove it in us. But that necessitates learning to live in dependence upon the Holy Spirit. Apart from that, failure is inevitable.

---

2. For a lucid amplification of this theme, see Watchman Nee, *The Normal Christian Life* (Fort Washington, Pa.: Christian Lit. Crusade, 1961). And for a helpful contemporary application of these principles, see Francis A. Schaeffer, *True Spirituality* (Wheaton: Tyndale, 1971).

Student-teacher clashes are not new. The dialogues of Plato make it clear that the students of Socrates were greatly irritated by their demanding teacher. Recently, I was asked to help resolve the tension between a group of Christian students and their doctrine professor. During the discussion, one of the students summed up the mood of our time in a single sentence, "I don't see why I have to sit in any class that doesn't turn me on," he offered. "I have a right to skip any class that isn't meaningful to me."

The accepted philosophy of today is existentialism, which, in its popular form, emphasizes meaningful experience as the criterion for truth. Facts are considered irrelevant, except insofar as they "turn us on." Jesus is popular in some groups, not necessarily because He is the only way to God, but because "You can get high on him," as the lapel buttons suggest. Many who have tried Christ have become disillusioned because they didn't get high, as they had expected. In terms of sheer thrills, some other substitute might do just as well. At least for a while.

Shouldn't the Christian life be more meaningful than any other experience, dogma, or religion? The answer depends on what you consider a meaningful life to be.

Let's look at Christ once more. He reminded His weary disciples, "My food is to do the will of Him that sent Me, and to accomplish His work" (Jn 4:34). The relationship with His Father was just as necessary as the food that nourished Him during those long walks in the blistering Palestinian sun.

The work that the Father asked the Son to do was

not exciting by itself. Washing the dusty feet of nearly a dozen men (possibly Judas did not permit Christ to wash his feet) would not give anyone a "spiritual high," as many Christians constantly expect. But Christ did not complain. He did not suggest that it was disgraceful that God the Son be on His hands and knees.

To Christ, it made little difference whether He was washing the disciples feet or preaching the Sermon on the Mount. The *type* of activity did not determine whether Christ was joyful or not. His joy was found in doing the will of God, and if that included washing feet, that was fine. All that He cared about was that He could say, "And He who sent Me is with Me; He has not left Me alone, for I always do the things that are pleasing to Him" (Jn 8:29). That was enough to give life purpose and joy.

Undoubtedly, doctrine courses need improvement, churches should be more relevant, and Christian homes more exciting. But as long as we believe that the answer to fulfillment lies in changes in methods, techniques, and a more meaningful approach to Christian life-styles, we have not diagnosed our malady correctly. Nothing, not even classes that turn us on, can be a substitute for finding fulfillment in God through the Scriptures He has given.

Here is the paradox: Christ found the horror of the cross a joy, because whatever pleased the Father, pleased Him (Heb 12:2). The fulfillment (or meaningfulness) of the Christian life is not necessarily found in the experiences we have (many of them will turn us off!), but even tragedies can have a glimmer of joy when we have the faith to see God's purpose in it all.

St. Augustine observed that God made us for Himself and our hearts are restless until they find their rest in Him. Learning this is not easy. A thousand voices clamor for our attention, and a thousand causes vie for our support. But until we have learned to be satisfied with fellowship with God, until He is our rock and our fortress, we will be restless with our place in the world.

Whenever my life lacks meaning, it is because I am seeking fulfillment somewhere apart from God and the Word. Then God disciplines me to bring me back to Him. I am only beginning to appreciate Christ's observation that to save one's life is to lose it; to lose it for Him is to find it.

But slowly, God's promises are being translated into power. There is hope for Karen. There is hope for you and for me. That is encouraging.

14

SO WHAT IF I AM WORLDLY?

ARE THE PRESSURES Christians face in today's world new? Yes. And no. It is true that no other generation has had to live with the influence of the mass media, sleek pornographic magazines, and X-rated movies. It is also true that technology has created new anxieties, polluted our air, and ushered in a host of distressing changes. Along with the knowledge explosion has come a radical shift in the moral climate. Many Christians find it so difficult to cope with this generation that they hope for the Lord's immediate return. Of course, such a hope should characterize believers of all ages, but one senses that many Christians long for the rapture, not because of their intense love for the Lord, but because it symbolizes an escape from the distress of our age.

Yet, our problems are not new. The components of worldliness, the struggles with the flesh and the devil, have always been part of Christian experience. Whether we retain our identity or are squeezed into the world's mold will depend largely on our individual relationship with God. For this reason, this book emphasizes our personal attitudes toward issues which clamor for a biblical answer.

Yet, as individuals, we must be concerned about the collective witness of the true Church. John Donne reminded us that no man is an island; one man's victory or failure affects us all. This is especially true among believers, because we are organically connected by the indwelling Spirit. Paul used the metaphor of the body to illustrate the interdependence of individual Christians (1 Co 12:12-13). When one part of our physical body suffers, the other parts suffer; when one part accomplishes its duty, it is always a cooperative effort.

Have you ever seen a human hand severed from a body? It looks gruesome. Yet, attached to an arm and connected to the nervous system, the hand is not only highly useful but beautiful too. The difference lies in its relationship to the body. Similarly, in Christ, no individual is *anything, cut off from the body.*

This interdependence results in a cooperative concern for the various parts of the body. What happens when you see an object hurtling through the air toward your head? Instinctively, your hand shields your head from the blow. Similarly, we as Christians are connected in Christ. When one Christian fails, we share his failure and care for his needs. When he is restored to fellowship, we rejoice with him.

We can't afford to believe that it doesn't matter whether we are actively involved in the struggles against the world or whether we are drifting aimlessly with the tide. When we lose our passion for the Church (Christ's Body) and are preoccupied with our own concerns, our witness will be submerged. We will drown in the icy waters of indifference.

Recent trends in America encourage us. Many evangelical churches are growing rapidly. Scores of laymen are beginning to see the challenge of witnessing for Christ in their vocations. The present emphasis on sharing and informal meetings (as opposed to the rigidity of some established churches) is healthy, if kept within New Testament guidelines. Furthermore, a greater number of evangelical books are being sold now than ever before. These developments are cause for thanksgiving.

Yet the influence of the Church in some segments of society is waning. In the face of moral perversion, political corruption, and purely secular attitudes, the voice of the Church is lost, or at least muffled. Ironically, secular groups (e.g., antiabortion coalitions) are fighting moral issues without much help from the evangelical Church. Long ago we left the dynamic of the early disciples who were accused of turning the world upside down. Tragically, it often is the world which has turned *us* upside down!

If history repeats itself (as it often does, at least in principle), the witness of the Church in America could eventually be obliterated.

An example of how this could happen comes from the records of history. From the second to the fourth centuries, Christianity spread rapidly throughout North Africa. Churches sprang up in rapid succession. An historian living in that day might well have guessed that Christianity would become the dominant religion in most of Africa. It was here that Tertullian (known as the flaming thunderer of North Africa) and Augustine, the famous apologist, exerted their influence. Yet, the church in North Africa, which began with such high hopes, was later obliterated. A few centuries later, scarcely a trace of Christianity could be found. Why? What elements are necessary for a church to be absorbed by the world?

For one thing, the internal problems of the church detracted it from its mission of reaching the world. During persecution, thousands yielded to the pressure and compromised their faith. Later, many of these sought readmission into the church. The Novatians and Donatists agreed that these deserters should be denied acceptance by the church. A host of others disagreed. This issue split the church for more than a century. Augustine tried to bring about a reconciliation but failed.

Divisions in a church are sometimes necessary. The purity of the Church has often been preserved by those who decide not to tolerate heresy or moral permissiveness. Yet, when the Church is torn by its own squabbles; when divisions exist continually, defeat for both sides is almost inevitable.

The same is true in the local church. A church preoccupied with its own differences or torn by schism is a good candidate for ultimate oblivion. In Ephesians 6, Paul describes the spiritual armor of the Christian. No provision is made for the Christian's back, not merely because he is never to turn and run in defeat, but also because it is assumed that he will not be fighting his comrades. If all of his energy is used in family battles, he will have neither the time nor the inclination to make an impact on the world.

The cure for this is compassion, understanding, and, above all, love. As pointed out earlier in this book, differences must be held without bitterness, self-righteousness, and pride. In this way, a church can work out its differences and exercise discipline without diminishing its impact on the world. Whenever we are preoccupied merely with our own survival, whenever we begin to entertain ourselves with our own quarrels the end might not be too far away.

Another factor in the decline of the church in North

Africa is the distinction made between the laity and the clergy. Iranaeus had taught that the apostles had appointed bishops as successors. Eusebius, the most famous of the early Church historians attempted to list the bishops of several churches. Soon every town had its bishop. These men began to grow in power; they were in charge of the worship and supervised the entire life of the church within their territorial jurisdiction. Cyprian, Bishop of Carthage and martyr in the third century, held that he who was not in the church was not a Christian and that outside the church there was no salvation. The belief then developed that the bishop had the authority to consecrate other bishops and ordain subordinate clergy. The New Testament teaching that every Christian is a priest before God was lost in an elaborate hierarchical system.

One of the greatest threats to the impact of the church is the belief that the clergy alone is responsible for spiritual matters. The clergy is hired to do the work of the ministry. Consequently, thousands of Christians do not even see it as their responsibility to serve God within the Church and witness to the world outside of it. They believe that attending church and listening to a sermon is the penalty they must pay for being a Christian. Beyond that, they have no vision, no ministry, no fulfillment. This is why the Church cannot be revived without individuals being renewed. As long as people come to worship at a structure (church) without learning to live on supernatural power, the Church will not survive for long. The next generation will already reveal the carnal fruit of stagnant religion.

A sharp cleavage between clergy and laity leads to the indifference of the laity; it also leads to the worldly attitudes of the clergy. In North Africa, the bishops began to use their spiritual authority to get political power. As the church and state became united, spiritual life was replaced with political arbitrations. Little wonder that New Testament Christianity soon vanished in North Africa.

This book stresses the fact that Christianity is more than a set of regulations imposed upon believers. It is possible to fit into Christian patterns without discovering Christian power. Often our churches are simply functioning because of the momentum generated by faithful men and women of the past. When this happens, we will eventually lose our impetus. The challenge comes to each one of us to join in the battle against the world's deceptive influence and to march with supernatural power. Ministers and missionaries cannot take our place in the struggle. Every believer (whether he realizes it or not) is involved in the conflict between good and evil, between God and the world. You and I dare not shirk our responsibility.

The church in North Africa declined for another reason: racial and social discrimination. A bishop of Carthage was consecrated in A.D. 311 by one who evidently was a traitor during the persecution. Another bishop was chosen by the Donatists. Yet, this split was not merely doctrinal. It was also racial. The Donatists were largely non-Latin; the Catholics were drawn from the Latin elements of the population. The Catholic element wished to preserve its power, and, as a result, Latin was the language of the religious elite. The Bible was not translated into the language of North Africa, and, by the time of the Vandal invasion in the fifth century, the light of the Gospel was practically extinguished.

Ironically, we twentieth-century Christians have not fully learned the lessons of history. When we appeal to one class or race to the exclusion of another, the Gospel's impact will be diluted. Frequently, minority groups have considered the Church as an enemy or at best an unconcerned friend. Why? Because our actions give the impression that Christ died only for those who resemble *us*. Consequently, some racial or social groups believe that Christianity—at least the Christianity they have seen—is not for them.

The Church grows only in proportion to its penetration into the world. Without new converts, individual witnessing, and loving concern for people, its impact on the world is lost. There are no shortcuts to evangelism and growth. We can perpetuate the status quo with our own plans and initiative. But we cannot change the world that way.

In A.D. 140, an anonymous Christian wrote a letter to Diognetus. In it, he described the Christian's relationship to the world:

> For Christians cannot be distinguished from the rest of the human race by country or language or customs. They do not live in cities of their own; they do not use a peculiar form of speech; they do not follow an eccentric manner of life. This doctrine of theirs has not been discovered by the ingenuity or deep thought of inquisitive men, nor do they put forward a merely human teaching, as some people do. Yet, although they live in Greek and barbarian cities alike, as each man's lot has been cast, and follow the customs of the country in clothing and food and other matters of daily living, at the same time they give proof of the remarkable and admittedly extraordinary constitution of their own commonweath. They live in their own

countries, but only as aliens. They have a share in everything as citizens, and endure everything as foreigners. Every foreign land is their fatherland, and yet for them every fatherland is a foreign land. . . . They busy themselves on earth but their citizenship is in heaven. They obey the established laws, but in their own lives they go far beyond what the laws require. They love all men, and by all men are persecuted. They are unknown, and still they are condemned; they are put to death, and yet they are brought to life. They are poor, and yet they make many rich; they are completely destitute, and yet they enjoy complete abundance. They are dishonored, and in their very dishonor are glorified; they are defamed and are vindicated. They are reviled, and yet they bless; when they are affronted, they still pay due respect. When they do good, they are punished as evildoers; undergoing punishment, they rejoice because they are brought to life. They are treated by the Jews as foreigners and enemies, and are hunted down by the Greeks; and all the time those who hate them find it impossible to justify their enmity. [Finally, in the conclusion of the letter, this Christian observed,] The soul, when faring badly as to food and drink, grows better; so too Christians, when punished, day by day increase more and more. It is to no less a post than this that God has ordered them, and they must not try to evade it.[1]

Let us join hands with the Christians throughout the centuries who did not abandon the task to which God had called them. And if God be for us, who can be against us?

---

1. "The So-called Letter to Diognetus" in *The Library of Christian Classics* (Philadelphia: Westminster, 1953) 1:216-18.